The Everyday Co Cookbook with 130 Recipes that are Easy on the Budget

by Vesela Tabakova
Text copyright(c)2016 Vesela Tabakova

All rights reserved. No part of this publication may be reproduced, distributed, or transmitted in any form or by any means, including photocopying, recording, or other electronic or mechanical methods, without the prior written permission of the publisher, except in the case of brief quotations embodied in critical reviews and certain other noncommercial uses permitted by copyright law.

Although every precaution has been taken to verify the accuracy of the information contained herein, the author and publisher assume no responsibility for any errors or omissions. No liability is assumed for damages that may result from the use of information contained within.

Dedication
To my Mom and Dad - Thank You!

Table Of Contents

Introduction	7
Chicken and Iceberg Lettuce Salad	11
Creamy Chicken and Pasta Salad	12
Cauliflower Salad	13
Beetroot and Carrot Salad with Salmon and Egg	14
Beet Salad with Yogurt	15
Beet and Lentil Salad	16
Shepherds' Salad	17
Fried Zucchinis with Yogurt Sauce	18
Spinach Stem Salad	19
Winter Salad	20
Roasted Leek and Sweet Potato Salad	21
Artichoke and Bean Salad with Lemon Mint Dressing	22
Artichoke and Mushroom Salad	23
Warm Vitamin Salad	24
Caprese Pasta Salad	25
Roasted Pepper Pasta Salad	26
Buckwheat Salad with Asparagus and Roasted Peppers	27
Roasted Broccoli Buckwheat Salad	28
Cheese Stuffed Tomatoes	29
Mozzarella, Tomato and Basil Couscous Salad	30
Soups	31
Chicken Soup with Rice	32
Lemon Chicken and Kale Soup	33
Slow Cooker French-style Farmhouse Chicken Soup	34
Chicken Vegetable Soup	35
Slow Cooker Chicken Noodle Soup	36
Chicken and Ricotta Meatball Soup	37
Asparagus and Chicken Soup	38
Asian-style Chicken Soup	39
Smoked Meat Russian Soup	40
Dump Bean and Bacon Soup	42
Fish and Noodle Soup	43
Hearty Lamb and Vegetable Soup	44
Slow Cooker Corn Chowder	45
Red Lentil and Quinoa Soup	46
Slow Cooker Summer Garden Soup	48
Cheesy Cauliflower Soup	49

Creamy Artichoke Soup	50
Lentil, Barley and Kale Soup	51
Spinach and Mushroom Soup	52
Simple Black Bean Soup	53
Lentil and Cabbage Soup	54
Sweet Potato Soup	55
Irish Carrot Soup	56
Spicy Carrot Soup	57
Main Dishes	58
Chicken with Almonds and Prunes	59
Sweet and Sour Sicilian Chicken	60
Carribean Chicken	61
Mexican Lime Chicken	62
Peanut Butter Dump Chicken	63
Blue Cheese and Mushroom Dump Chicken	64
Pesto Chicken	65
Greek Chicken And Lemon Rice	66
Spicy Chicken and Bean Stew	68
Mediterranean Chicken Stew	69
Slow Cooker Herb Chicken and Vegetables	70
Chicken With Spinach and Mushrooms	71
Lemon-spiced Chicken with Chickpeas	72
Honey Mustard Chicken with Parsnips	73
Andalusian Style Chicken	74
Portuguese Style Chicken	76
Slow Cooked Chicken with Tomatoes and Artichokes	77
Homemade Lasagna	78
Beef and Spinach Lasagna	80
Mediterranean Bolognaise	81
Ground Beef Pasta with Yogurt Sauce	82
Baked Ground Beef Pasta	83
Beef Stew with Green Peas	84
Potato Beef Stew	85
Beef with Mushrooms	86
Beef and Spinach Stew	87
Beef and Okra Stew	88
Mixed Vegetables with Beef	89
Stuffed Tomatoes with Bulgur and Ground Beef	90
Stuffed Artichokes	92
Stuffed Cabbage Leaves with Ground Beef and Rice	93

Meatballs with Parsley Sauce	95
Meatballs with Egg-lemon Sauce	96
Spinach with Ground Beef	98
Ground Beef and Chickpea Casserole	99
Greek Lamb Stew	100
Hearty Lamb Stew	101
Sweet Spiced Lamb Shanks With Quince	102
Slow Cooked Lamb with Red Wine Sauce	104
Slow Cooked Mediterranean Lamb	105
Slow Cooked Lamb with Lemon, Dill and Feta	106
Slow Cooked Beef Couscous	107
Beef and Root Vegetable Crock Pot	109
One-pot Pork Chops With Fennel and Potatoes	110
Pork Chops with Balsamic Roasted Vegetables	111
Juicy Pork Chops	113
One-pot Pork with Orange and Olives	114
Mediterranean Pork Casserole	115
Pork Roast and Cabbage	116
Turkey Sausage and Lentil One-pot	117
Sausage and Vegetable One-pot	118
Mediterranean Baked Fish	119
Eggplant and Chickpea Stew	120
Eggplant Stew	121
Squash, Lentil and Bean One-pot	122
Maple Roast Parsnip with Pear and Sage	124
Balsamic Roasted Carrots and Baby Onions	125
Summer Pasta Bake	126
Mediterranean Vegetable Casserole	127
Baked Mediterranean Casserole with Tofu and Feta Cheese	128
Okra and Tomato Casserole	129
Zucchinis with Chickpeas and Rice	130
Zucchini Fritters	131
Spinach with Eggs	132
Breakfasts and Desserts	133
Sausage, Egg and Tomato Sandwiches	134
Grilled Chicken and Mozarella Toast	135
Grilled Egg and Feta Toast	136
Italian Beef Sandwiches	137
Sausage, Tomato and Cheese Sandwiches	138
Eggs Baked in Tomato Sauce	139

Mediterranean Scrambled Eggs	140
Salami Scrambled Eggs	141
Mushroom and Spinach Scrambled Eggs	142
Feta and Olive Scrambled Eggs	143
Cornmeal Avocado Muffins	144
Healthy Breakfast Muffins	145
Marmalade Muffins	147
Semolina Dessert	149
Coconut-flavored Rice Pudding with Figs	150
Pasta with Honey and Pistachios	151
Yogurt-Strawberry Ice Pops	152
Blueberry Yogurt Dessert	153
Date Pinwheels	154
Date and Walnut Cookies	156
Turkish Delight Cookies	157
FREE BONUS RECIPES: 10 Natural Homemade Body Scrubs and Beauty Recipes	158
About the Author	169

Introduction

In my family we are no strangers to stretching the dollar, living in an ex-Communist country that is still one of the poorest within the EU. We are always living paycheck to paycheck, so we find the cheapest ways possible to cook meals that will feed our family of five. Our menus are strongly influenced by traditional cuisine and contain a lot of simple, hearty foods. When I think about it, every meal in my house is a comfort food and is also cooked with the budget in mind.

Some of our favorite recipes are those inexpensive dishes that we had at home when we were growing up, like Roast Chicken, Chicken and Potatoes, Chicken with Lemon Rice, Green Salad, Feta Cheese Stuffed Tomatoes, Summer Pasta Bake, Greek Lamb Stew, Stuffed Peppers or Meatballs in Parsley Sauce. So today, these meals are frequently on our table and are especially loved by our kids.

There are several ways we stretch the dollar. We make a lot more soups, casseroles and one pot dinners, bean and rice dishes, or stewed vegetables with rice. We also have one or two vegetarian dinners each week because Bulgarian vegetarian food is incredibly healthy, cheap and easy to cook.

We try to buy produce that is seasonally available and, when possible, buy in bulk. We eat lots of greens, potatoes, squash, cabbage and other less pricey vegetables, prepared in a variety of ways. Lentils, beans, green peas and chickpeas, are all inexpensive and the recipes to prepare them are also endless. Herbs and spices are a great way to enhance the flavor of a dish without having to spend much at all. The spices we use are not expensive but would be even cheaper if you grow them in pots at your kitchen window.

Another thing to do is buy meat only when on sale and stock up the freezer. We frequently cook egg dishes, meatloaf, meatballs, or different Mediterranean meat and fish recipes that are not only delicious but also budget friendly and healthy.

And because it is not good to throw away food, don't forget to use your leftover fruits and vegetables for health and beauty routines. If an avocado or banana has gone too ripe, use it as a hair or face mask. After saving all this money on food, you deserve a little pampering!

Cooking on a budget doesn't mean you have to sacrifice flavor or nutrition. Cooking on a budget is a skill you learn over time. Yes, it takes a little more time and planning but in the end it turns out that the more you focus on purchasing local, unprocessed food and preparing meals at home, the healthier and tastier your meals will be, and the more money you'll save.

Salads and Appetizers

Balsamic Chicken and White Bean Salad

Serves 4-6

Ingredients:

1 lb skinless chicken breasts

1 cup canned white beans, drained

1 cup cherry tomatoes, halved

1 cup feta cheese, crumbled

1 cup rocket leaves

2 garlic cloves, crushed

1 tbsp honey

2 tbsp balsamic vinegar

3 tbsp olive oil

Directions:

Whisk garlic, honey and vinegar in a deep bowl. Add chicken breasts and turn to coat. Season with salt and black pepper to taste. Cover and marinate for thirty minutes.

Preheat a barbecue plate or grill on high heat. Lightly brush chicken with oil and cook for two minutes each side or until golden.

Reduce heat to medium-low and cook chicken for five minutes each side or until cooked through. Set aside in a plate, covered, for five minutes then slice.

Combine beans, tomatoes, feta cheese, rocket leaves and chicken in a salad bowl. Toss gently and serve.

Chicken and Iceberg Lettuce Salad

Serves 6-7

Ingredients:

2 cups cooked chicken, coarsely chopped

1/2 head iceberg lettuce, halved and chopped

1 celery rib, chopped

1 big apple, peeled and chopped

1/2 red bell pepper, deseeded and chopped

9-10 green olives, pitted and halved

1 red onion, sliced

for the dressing:

2 tbsp olive oil

1 tbsp honey

2 tbsp lemon juice

salt and pepper, to taste

Directions:

Cut all the vegetables and toss them, together with the olives, in a large bowl. Chop the already cooked and cooled chicken into small pieces and add it to the salad.

Prepare the salad dressing in a separate smaller bowl by mixing together the olive oil, honey and lemon juice. Season with salt and pepper, to taste, and serve.

Creamy Chicken and Pasta Salad

Serves 4

Ingredients:

2 cups small pasta, cooked

2 chicken breast halves, cooked and diced

1 cup cherry tomatoes, halved

1/2 cup green olives, pitted and halved

1 red pepper, chopped

1/2 red onion, sliced

3 tbsp low-fat crème fraîche

2 tbsp mayonnaise

salt, to taste

Directions:

Place pasta, chicken, tomatoes, olives, red onion and red pepper in a salad bowl.

Mix the mayonnaise and crème fraîche and combine with the pasta, vegetables and chicken.

Cauliflower Salad

Serves 5-6

Ingredients:

3 cups small cauliflower florets

1/3 cup Greek yogurt

2-3 garlic cloves, chopped

3 tbsp finely cut dill

1/2 cup crushed walnuts

3 tbsp extra virgin olive oil

salt and freshly ground black pepper, to taste

Directions:

In a skillet, heat the olive oil and cook the cauliflower florets for 10 minutes, or until they are cooked through and tender.

Combine the yogurt, garlic, dill and walnuts. Season with salt and pepper to taste.

Place the cauliflower in a salad bowl. Pour over the yogurt mixture and serve.

Beetroot and Carrot Salad with Salmon and Egg

Serves 4

Ingredients:

3 eggs, boiled and quartered

2 beets, peeled and coarsely grated

2 carrots, peeled and coarsely grated

5 oz smoked salmon, flaked

3-4 green onions, chopped

1/4 cup fresh lemon juice

2 tbsp olive oil

salt and black pepper, to taste

Directions:

Boil eggs over high heat for 5 minutes. Drain, cool and peel.

Shred carrots and beets and divide them among serving plates. Cut each egg in quarters and place on top of the vegetables. Top with the salmon flakes.

Prepare the dressing by whisking lemon juice and oil in a small bowl. Season with salt and pepper and drizzle the dressing over the salad. Serve sprinkled with green onions.

Beet Salad with Yogurt

Serves 4

Ingredients:

3 medium beets

1 cup strained yogurt

2 garlic cloves, crushed

1 tsp white wine vine vinegar or lemon juice

1 tbsp olive oil

1/2 tsp dried mint

½ tsp salt

Directions:

Wash beets, cut the stems and steam them in a pot for 25-30 minutes, or until cooked through.

When they cool down, peel and dry with a paper towel then grate and place them in a deep salad bowl. Add in the other ingredients and toss. Serve cold.

Beet and Lentil Salad

Serves 6

Ingredients:

1 can brown lentils, drained and rinsed

1 can pickled beets, drained and cut in cubes

5 oz baby rocket leaves

¼ cup walnuts, toasted and roughly chopped

4-5 green onions, chopped

1 garlic clove, crushed

3 tbsp olive oil

2 tbsp lemon juice

salt and black pepper, to taste

Directions:

Heat olive oil in a frying pan and gently sauté the green onions for 1-2 minutes or until softened. Add in garlic and lentils. Cook, for 2 minutes the add in beets and cook for 2-3 minutes more.

Combine baby rocket, walnuts and lentil mixture in a large salad bowl. Sprinkle with lemon juice, toss gently to combine and serve.

Shepherds' Salad

Serves 6-8

Ingredients:

5-6 tomatoes, sliced

2 cucumbers, peeled and sliced

5-6 white mushrooms, sliced

2 red bell peppers, sliced

7 oz ham, diced

1 onion, sliced

3 eggs, boiled and sliced

7 oz feta cheese, grated

1/2 bunch parsley, finely cut

4 tbsp olive oil

1 tbsp red wine vinegar

1 tsp salt

20-30 black olives

Directions:

Slice the tomatoes, cut the cucumbers, peppers and onion, thinly slice the mushrooms. Dice the ham.

Combine all ingredients in a salad bowl and drizzle with olive oil and vinegar. Season with salt and mix well.

Divide the salad in plates and sprinkle with feta cheese and parsley. Top with egg slices and olives. Serve chilled.

Fried Zucchinis with Yogurt Sauce

Serves 4

Ingredients:

4 medium zucchinis

2 cups yogurt

3 cloves garlic, crushed

a bunch of fresh dill, chopped

1 cup sunflower oil

1 cup flour

salt

Directions:

Start by combining the garlic and chopped dill with the yogurt in a bowl. Add salt to taste and put in the fridge.

Wash and peel the zucchinis, and cut them in thin diagonal slices or in rings 1/4 in thick. Salt and leave them in a suitable bowl placing it inclined to drain away the juices.

Coat the zucchinis with flour, then fry turning on both sides until they are golden-brown (about 3 minutes on each side).

Transfer to paper towels and pat dry. Serve the zucchinis hot or cold, with the yogurt mixture on the side.

Spinach Stem Salad

Serves 1-2

Ingredients:

a few bunches of spinach stems

water to boil the stems

1 garlic clove, minced

lemon juice or vinegar, to taste

olive oil

salt, to taste

Directions:

Trim the stems so that they will remain intact. Wash the stems very well. Steam stems in a basket over boiling water for 2 to 3 minutes until wilted but not too fluffy.

Place them on a plate and sprinkle with minced garlic, olive oil, lemon juice or vinegar, and salt.

Winter Salad

Serves 5-6

Ingredients:

2 small bees, peeled, boiled and grated

2 gherkins, chopped

2 boiled eggs, grated

2 boiled potatoes, grated

3-4 spring onions, finely cut

1/2 cup mayonnaise

salt and black pepper to taste

Directions:

Place beets, gherkins, eggs, potatoes and spring onions in a salad bowl. Stir in mayonnaise.

Season with salt and black pepper to taste and serve.

Roasted Leek and Sweet Potato Salad

Serves 5

Ingredients:

1 lb sweet potato, unpeeled, cut into 1 inch pieces

3-4 leeks, trimmed and cut into 1 inch slices

a handful of baby spinach leaves

1 cup watercress, rinsed, patted dry and separated from roots

1 tbsp dried mint

2 tbsp olive oil

2 tbsp lemon juice

Directions:

Preheat oven to 350 F. Line a baking tray with baking paper and place the sweet potato and leeks on it. Drizzle with olive oil and sprinkle with mint. Toss to coat. Roast for 20 minutes or until tender.

Place roasted vegetables, baby spinach and watercress in a salad bowl and stir. Sprinkle with lemon juice and serve.

Artichoke and Bean Salad with Lemon Mint Dressing

Serves 5

Ingredients:

1 can white beans, drained

2/3 cup podded broad beans

4 marinated artichoke hearts, quartered

2/3 cup diced green bell pepper

for the dressing:

3 tbsp olive oil

3 tbsp lemon juice

1 tsp dried mint

5-6 fresh mint leaves, very finely cut

salt and pepper, to taste

Directions:

Boil the broad beans in unsalted water for 3-4 minutes or until tender. Drain and hold under running cold water for a few minutes.

Combine with the canned beans, bell peppers and quartered marinated artichoke hearts in a deep salad bowl.

In a small bowl, mix olive oil, lemon juice, dried mint and fresh mint.whisk until smooth. Add in salt and pepper and pour over salad. Toss gently to combine and serve.

Artichoke and Mushroom Salad

Serves: 4-5

Prep time: 15 min

Ingredients:

1 oz can artichoke hearts, drained, cut quartered

7-8 white mushrooms, chopped

1 red pepper, chopped

1/3 cup chopped black olives

1 tbsp capers

3 tbsp lemon juice

2 tbsp olive oil

salt and pepper, to taste

Directions:

Place the artichokes and mushrooms in a large salad bowl and stir to mix well. Add in olives, capers and red pepper and toss to combine.

In a small bowl, whisk the lemon juice and olive oil until smooth. Pour over the salad, toss and serve.

Warm Vitamin Salad

Serves 4

Ingredients:

7 oz cauliflower, cut into florets

7 oz baby Brussels sprouts, trimmed

7 oz broccoli, cut into florets

1/2 cup chopped leeks

for the dressing:

2 tbsp lemon juice

2 tbsp olive oil

1/2 tsp ginger powder

1/2 cup parsley leaves, very finely cut

Directions:

Cook cauliflower, broccoli and Brussels sprouts in a steamer basket over boiling water for 10 minutes or until just tender. Refresh under cold water for a minute and set aside in a deep salad bowl.

Whisk the lemon juice, olive oil and ginger powder in a small bowl. Add in salt and pepper to taste; pour over the salad. Top with parsley and serve.

Caprese Pasta Salad

Serves 5-6

Ingredients:

2 cups cooked small pasta

1 cup baby mozzarella

2 cups cherry tomatoes, halved

4 tbsp basil pesto

3 tbsp white balsamic vinegar

2 tbsp olive oil

a bunch of baby arugula leaves, to serve

Directions:

Cook pasta as directed on package. Remove from heat, drain and rinse.

Combine pesto, olive oil and vinegar in a small cup.

Place tomatoes, mozzarella, and pasta in a salad bowl. Season with salt and pepper. Stir in pesto mixture. Toss to combine, top with arugula and serve.

Roasted Pepper Pasta Salad

Serves: 4-5

Prep time: 30 min

Ingredients:

12 oz small pasta

2 red peppers, halved and de-seeded

2 yellow peppers, halved and de-seeded

1 cup cherry tomatoes

3-4 garlic cloves, sliced

3 tbsp olive oil

2 tbsp sugar

1/2 cup finely chopped parsley leaves

Parmesan cheese, to serve

Directions:

Line a baking tray and place the peppers, tomatoes and garlic on it. Sprinkle with olive oil and sugar and season with salt and black pepper to taste.

Roast in a preheated to 375 F oven for 20 minutes, or until the vegetables are slightly charred around the edges.

Cook the pasta according to package directions. Combine it with the roasted vegetables and serve with parsley and Parmesan cheese.

Buckwheat Salad with Asparagus and Roasted Peppers

Serves 4-5

Ingredients:

1 cup buckwheat groats

1 3/4 cups vegetable broth

1/2 lb asparagus, trimmed and cut into 1 in pieces

4 roasted red bell peppers, diced

2-3 spring onions, finely chopped

2 garlic cloves, crushed

1 tbsp red wine vinegar

3 tbsp olive oil

salt and black pepper, to taste

1/2 cup fresh parsley leaves, finely cut

Directions:

Heat a large, dry saucepan and toast the buckwheat for about three minutes. Boil the vegetable broth and add it carefully to the buckwheat. Cover, reduce heat and simmer until buckwheat is tender and all liquid is absorbed (five-seven minutes). Remove from heat, fluff with a fork and set aside to cool.

Rinse out the saucepan and then bring about an inch of water to a boil. Cook the asparagus in a steamer basket or colander, two to three minutes until tender.

Transfer the asparagus in a large bowl along with the roasted peppers. Add in the spring onions, garlic, red wine vinegar, salt, pepper and olive oil. Stir to combine. Add the buckwheat to the vegetable mixture. Sprinkle with parsley and toss the salad gently.

Roasted Broccoli Buckwheat Salad

Serves 4-5

Ingredients:

1 cup buckwheat groats

1 3/4 cups water

1 head of broccoli, cut into small pieces

1 lb asparagus, trimmed and cut into 1 in pieces

1/2 cup roasted cashews

1/2 cup basil leaves, minced

1/2 cup olive oil

2 garlic cloves, crushed

3 tbsp Parmesan cheese, grated, to serve

Directions:

Arrange vegetables on a baking sheet and drizzle with olive oil. Roast in a preheated to 350 F oven for about fifteen minutes or until tender.

Heat a large, dry saucepan and toast the buckwheat for about three minutes, or until it releases a nutty aroma. Boil the water and add it carefully to the buckwheat.

Cover, reduce heat and simmer until the buckwheat is tender and all liquid is absorbed (five-seven minutes). Remove from heat, fluff with a fork and set aside to cool.

Prepare the dressing by blending basil leaves, olive oil, garlic, and salt.

Toss vegetables, buckwheat and dressing together in a salad bowl. Add in cashews and serve sprinkled with Parmesan cheese.

Cheese Stuffed Tomatoes

Serves 4

Ingredients:

4 large tomatoes

9 oz feta cheese

1 tsp paprika

Directions:

Cut the top of each tomato in such a way as to be able to stuff the tomato and cover with the cap. Scoop out the seeds and central part of the tomatoes to create a hollow.

Mash the scooped out parts of the tomatoes, add to the feta cheese and stir to make a homogeneous mixture. Add paprika. Stuff the tomatoes with the mixture and cover with the caps. Serve chilled, garnished with sprays of parsley.

Mozzarella, Tomato and Basil Couscous Salad

Serves 4

Ingredients:

4 tomatoes, diced

1 cup fresh mozzarella cheese, diced

3-4 spring onions, very finely cut

2 tbsp olive oil

1 tbsp lemon juice

salt, to taste

1/4 teaspoon fresh ground black pepper

1 garlic clove, crushed

1 cup couscous

1 1/4 cups water

1/2 cup chopped fresh basil

Directions:

In a big salad bowl combine tomatoes, mozzarella, salt, pepper, garlic, lemon juice, olive oil and spring onions. Toss everything well, cover, and marinate for half an hour.

Boil the water and pour over the couscous. Set aside for five minutes then fluff with a fork. Add couscous to the tomato mixture along with the chopped basil leaves and toss again.

Soups

Chicken Soup with Rice

Serves 4

Ingredients:

1 lb boneless chicken thighs, cut in bite sized pieces

1/4 cup rice, rinsed

1 small onion, finely cut

2 carrots, grated

1 celery rib, finely cut

5 cups water

2 garlic cloves, chopped

1 bay leaf

1 tsp salt

1/2 tsp black pepper

1/2 cup fresh parsley, finely cut, to serve

4 tbsp lemon juice, to serve

Directions:

Heat a soup pot over medium heat. Gently sauté onion, garlic, carrot and celery, stirring occasionally.

Add in chicken, water and bay leaf and bring to a boil. Simmer for 10 minutes then season with salt and black pepper and add in rice. Stir to combine and simmer for 15 minutes more. Remove the bay leaf and serve with parsley and lemon juice.

Lemon Chicken and Kale Soup

Serves 5-6

Ingredients:

1 cup cooked chicken, cubed or shredded

1 small onion, chopped

1 small carrot, grated

1 bunch kale, cut into 1 inch pieces

4 cups chicken broth

1 tsp Worcestershire sauce

1 tsp Dijon mustard

3 tbsp olive oil

1 tsp paprika

3 tbsp lemon juice

1 tsp grated lemon zest

salt and black pepper, to taste

grated Parmezan cheese, to serve

Directions:

Heat a soup pot over medium heat. Gently sauté onion, garlic and carrot, stirring occasionally. Stir in the lemon zest, chicken broth, Worcestershire sauce, Dijon mustard and cooked chicken.

Bring to a boil then reduce heat and simmer for 10 minutes. Stir in the kale and simmer for 3-4 minutes or until kale is tender.

Stir in the lemon juice and season with salt and pepper to taste. Serve sprinkled with Parmezan cheese.

Slow Cooker French-style Farmhouse Chicken Soup

Serves 5-6

Ingredients:

4 skinless, boneless chicken thighs, cut into bite-sized pieces

1 leek, trimmed, halved, finely cut

1 celery rib, trimmed, halved, finely cut

2 carrots, chopped

1 fennel bulb, trimmed, diced

1 cup frozen peas

4 cups chicken broth

1 tsp thyme

1 tsp salt

Directions:

Combine all ingredients in the slow cooker. Cover and cook on low for 6-7 hours.

Chicken Vegetable Soup

Serves 6-7

Ingredients:

2 lb boneless chicken thighs, cut in bite sized pieces

1 small onion, chopped

1 celery rib, chopped

1/2 small parsnip, chopped

3 garlic cloves, chopped

1 carrot, chopped

1 red bell pepper, chopped

1 lb potatoes, peeled and cubed

5 cups chicken broth

1 tsp thyme

2 bay leaves

1 tsp salt

black pepper, to taste

1 tsp summer savory

Directions:

Season the chicken well with salt, ground black pepper and summer savory. Place it in a slow cooker with all remaining ingredients.

Cover and cook on low for 6-7 hours or on high for 4 hours.

Slow Cooker Chicken Noodle Soup

Serves 6-7

Ingredients:

2 lb boneless chicken thighs, cut in bite sized pieces

1 small onion, chopped

1 tomato, diced

1 red bell pepper, chopped

2-3 broccoli florets

4 cups chicken broth

2 cups wide egg noodles, uncooked

1 tsp garlic powder

1 tsp oregano

2 bay leaves

1 tsp salt

black pepper, to taste

Directions:

Season the chicken well with salt, black pepper garlic powder and oregano. Place it in a slow cooker with all remaining ingredients.

Cover and cook on low for 6-7 hours or on high for 4-5 hours.

Add noodles to slow cooker; cover and cook on low 20 minutes.

Chicken and Ricotta Meatball Soup

Serves 4-5

Ingredients:

1 lb ground chicken meat

1 egg, lightly whisked

1 cup whole milk ricotta

1 cup grated Parmezan cheese

2-3 tbsp flour

1/2 onion, chopped

4 cups chicken broth

2 cups baby spinach

1/2 tsp dried oregano

3 tbsp olive oil

½ tsp black pepper

Directions:

Place ground chicken, Ricotta, Parmezan, egg and black pepper in a bowl. Combine well with hands and roll teaspoonfuls of the mixture into balls. Roll each meatball in the flour then set aside on a large plate.

In a deep soup pot, heat olive oil and gently sauté onion until transparent. Add in oregano and chicken broth and bring to a boil. Add meatballs, reduce heat, and simmer, uncovered, for 15 minutes. Add baby spinach leaves and simmer for 2 more minutes until it wilts.

Asparagus and Chicken Soup

Serves 4

Ingredients:

5 cups chicken broth

2 leeks, finely cut

2 chicken breast fillets, cooked and shredded

1 bunch asparagus, trimmed and cut

1/2 cup parsley, finely chopped

salt and black pepper, to taste

lemon juice, to serve

Directions:

Heat the chicken broth in a large soup pot. Add in the shredded chicken and the leeks and bring to the boil.

Reduce heat and simmer for 5 minutes. Add the asparagus, parsley, salt and black pepper and cook for 2 minutes more. Serve with lemon juice.

Asian-style Chicken Soup

Serves 4-5

Ingredients:

1 roasted chicken, skin and bones removed, shredded

1/2 Chinese cabbage, shredded

5 cups chicken broth

1 cup water

1 red chilli, thinly sliced

2 carrots, peeled and cut into short, thin sticks

4 oz fresh shiitake mushrooms, sliced

16 oz snow peas, shredded lengthways

2 tbsp soy sauce

1/4 cup coriander leaves, finely cut

Directions:

Combine the chicken broth, water, soy sauce and the chilli in a deep soup pot. Gently bring to a boil then add in carrots, mushrooms, snow peas and shredded chicken.

Reduce heat and simmer for 3-4 minutes. Add the cabbage and cook for 2 minutes or until the cabbage wilts. Stir the coriander into soup. Divide soup between bowls and serve.

Smoked Meat Russian Soup

Serves 4

Ingredients:

3 cups chicken broth

2 cups water

1 onion, finely cut

1 large potato, diced

1 large carrot, grated

2 oz bacon, chopped

3 oz smoked pork sausage, chopped

5 oz smoked chicken breast, cubed

2 pickled cucumbers, chopped

3 tbsp tomato purée

1 tsp paprika

lemon juice, to serve

black olives, chopped, to serve

finely chopped parsnip, to serve

black pepper, to serve

Directions:

Combine the chicken broth and water in a deep soup pot and slowly bring to the boil.

In a deep frying pan, cook sausage, bacon and chicken breast for 3-4 minutes, then add in onion and carrot and cook for 2-3 minutes more, stirring constantly. Add in chopped pickled cucumbers, stir, and cook for 5 minutes. Add tomato purée and paprika, stir, and remove from heat.

Cut the potato and add it to the boiling broth. Let it simmer for 5 minutes then add in the fried meat and all other ingredients. Cook on low heat for 10 minutes then serve sprinkled with chopped olives, parsnip and lemon juice.

Dump Bean and Bacon Soup

Serves 5-6

Ingredients:

1 slices bacon, chopped

1 can Black Beans, rinsed

1 can Kidney Beans, rinsed

1 celery rib, chopped

1/2 red onion, chopped

1 can tomatoes, diced, undrained

4 cups water

1 tsp smoked paprika

1 tsp dried mint

1/2 cup fresh parsley

ground black pepper, to taste

Directions:

Dump all ingredients in a soup pot. Stir well and bring to a boil. Reduce heat and simmer for 35 minutes.

Season with salt and black pepper to taste, and serve.

Fish and Noodle Soup

Serves 4-5

Ingredients:

14 oz firm white fish, cut into strips

2 carrots, cut into ribbons

1 zucchini, cut into thin ribbons

7 oz white button mushrooms, sliced

1 celery rib, finely cut

1 cup baby spinach

7 oz fresh noodles

3 cups chicken broth

2 cups water

2 tbsp soy sauce

1/2 tsp ground ginger

black pepper, to taste

Directions:

Place chicken broth, water and soy sauce in a large saucepan. Bring to a boil and add in carrots, celery, zucchini, mushrooms, ginger and noodles.

Cook, partially covered, for 3-4 minutes then add in fish and simmer for 3 minutes or until the fish is cooked through. Add baby spinach and simmer, stirring, for 1 minute, or until it wilts. Season with black pepper and serve.

Hearty Lamb and Vegetable Soup

Serves 6-7

Ingredients:

2 cups roasted lamb, shredded

3 cups chicken or vegetable broth

1 cup water

1 cup canned tomatoes, diced, undrained

1 onion, chopped

1 large carrot, chopped

1 small turnip, chopped

1 celery rib

3 tbsp olive oil

salt and black pepper, to taste

Directions:

Gently heat olive oil in a large saucepan and sauté onion, carrot, celery and turnip, stirring, for 5 minutes, or until softened.

Add in lamb, broth, tomatoes, and a cup of water. Bring to the boil then reduce heat and simmer for 20 minutes, or until vegetables are tender. Season with salt and black pepper to taste.

Slow Cooker Corn Chowder

Serves 4

Ingredients:

1 can whole kernel corn, undrained

1 small onion, finely chopped

2 potatoes, peeled and cubed

1 cup diced ham

1 celery stalk, chopped

3 cups vegetable broth

2 cups water

1 can evaporated milk

2-3 fresh coriander sprigs, to serve

Directions:

In a slow cooker, place the potatoes, onions, ham, celery, corn, salt and pepper to taste. Add vegetable broth.

Cook on low setting for 7-8 hours and then stir in the evaporated milk. Cook for 40 more minutes and serve topped with finely cut coriander leaves.

Red Lentil and Quinoa Soup

Serves 4-5

Ingredients:

½ cup quinoa

1 cup red lentils

5 cups water

1 onion, chopped

2-3 garlic cloves, chopped

1 red bell pepper, finely cut

1 small tomato, chopped

3 tbsp olive oil

1 tsp ginger

1 tsp cummin

1 tbsp paprika

salt and black pepper, to taste

Directions:

Rinse quinoa and lentils very well in a fine mesh strainer under running water and set aside to drain.

In a large soup pot, heat the olive oil over medium heat. Add the onion, garlic and red pepper and sauté for 1-2 minutes until just fragrant.

Stir in paprika, spices, red lentils and quinoa. Add in water and gently bring to a boil then lower heat and simmer, covered, for 30 minutes.

Add the chopped tomato and salt and cook for 5 minutes more.

Blend the soup and serve.

Slow Cooker Summer Garden Soup

Serves 4-5

Ingredients:

1 small onion, finely cut

2 carrots, chopped

1 zucchini, peeled and cubed

1 box frozen baby lima beans, thawed

1 celery rib, thinly sliced

2 garlic cloves, chopped

4 cups vegetable broth

1 can tomatoes, diced, undrained

1 medium yellow summer squash, cubed

1 cup uncooked small pasta

3-4 tbsp pesto

black pepper and salt, to taste

Directions:

Add all ingredients except zucchini, summer squash and pasta into slow cooker. Cover and cook on low for 6 hours or high for 4 hours.

Stir in pasta, zucchini and yellow squash. Cover; cook 1 hour longer or until vegetables are tender. Top individual servings with pesto.

Cheesy Cauliflower Soup

Serves 4-5

Ingredients:

1 large onion, finely cut

1 medium head cauliflower, chopped

2-3 garlic cloves, minced

4 cups vegetable broth

1 cup whole cream

1 cup cheddar cheese, grated

salt, to taste

fresh ground black pepper, to taste

Directions:

Put cauliflower, onion, garlic and vegetable broth in crock pot. Cover and cook on low for 4-6 hours. Blend in a blender.

Return to crockpot and blend in cream and cheese. Season with salt and pepper and stir to mix.

Creamy Artichoke Soup

Serves 4

Ingredients:

1 can artichoke hearts, drained

3 potatoes, peeled and cut into ½-inch pieces

1 small onion, finely cut

2 cloves garlic, crushed

3 cups vegetable broth

2 tbsp lemon juice

1 cup heavy cream

black pepper, to taste

Directions:

Combine the potatoes, onion, artichoke hearts, broth, lemon juice and black pepper in the slow cooker.

Cover and cook on low for 8-10 hours or on high for 4-5 hours or until the potatoes are tender.

Blend the soup in batches and return it to the slow cooker. Add the cream and continue to cook until heated 5-10 minutes more. Garnish with a swirl of cream or a sliver of artichoke.

Lentil, Barley and Kale Soup

Serves 4

Ingredients:

2 medium leeks, chopped

2 garlic cloves, chopped

2 bay leaves

1 can tomatoes, diced and undrained

1/2 cup red lentils

1/2 cup barley

1 bunch kale, coarsely chopped

4 cups vegetable broth

3 tbsp olive oil

1 tbsp paprika

½ tsp cumin

Directions:

Heat olive oil in a large saucepan over medium-high heat and sauté leeks and garlic until fragrant. Add in cumin, paprika, tomatoes, lentils, barley and vegetable broth. Season with salt and pepper.

Cover, and bring to a boil then reduce heat and simmer for 40 minutes or until barley is tender. Add in kale and let it simmer for a few minutes more until it wilts.

Spinach and Mushroom Soup

Serves 4-5

Ingredients:

1 small onion, finely cut

1 small carrot, chopped

1 small zucchini, peeled and diced

1 medium potato, peeled and diced

6-7 white button mushrooms, chopped

2 cups chopped fresh spinach

4 cups vegetable broth or water

4 tbsp olive oil

salt and black pepper, to taste

Directions:

Heat olive oil in a large soup pot over medium heat. Add in potato, onion and mushroom and cook until vegetables are soft but not mushy.

Add chopped fresh spinach, the zucchini and vegetable broth and simmer for about 15 minutes. Season to taste with salt and pepper and serve.

Simple Black Bean Soup

Serves 5-6

Ingredients:

1 cup dried black beans

5 cups vegetable broth

1 large onion, chopped

1 red pepper, chopped

1 tsp sweet paprika

1 tbsp dried mint

2 bay leaves

1 serrano chile, finely chopped

1 tsp salt

4 tbsp fresh lime juice

1/2 cup chopped fresh cilantro

1 cup sour cream or yogurt, to serve

Directions:

Wash the beans and soak them in enough water overnight.

In a slow cooker, combine the beans and all other ingredients except for the lime juice and cilantro. Cover and cook on low for 7-8 hours.

Add salt, lime juice and fresh cilantro.

Serve with a dollop of sour cream or yogurt.

Lentil and Cabbage Soup

Serves 6-7

Ingredients:

1 cup dry lentils

1/2 onion, finely cut

2 carrots, cut

1 celery rib, chopped

1/2 head cabbage, sliced

2 garlic cloves, crushed

3 cups vegetable broth

1 cup water

2 tbsp olive oil

1 tbsp savory

1 tsp paprika

salt and pepper, to taste

Directions:

In a large soup pot, heat olive oil over medium-high heat and gently sauté onion and garlic for a minute or two. Add in celery, carrots and cook for an addition 2 minutes.

Once the onion is tender, add paprika, savory, dry lentils and stir well. Stir in 3 cups of vegetable broth, and 1 cup water.

Bring soup to a boil, add cabbage, lower heat, and simmer for about 30-40 minutes, or until the cabbage is tender.

Sweet Potato Soup

Serves 6-7

Ingredients:

2 lb sweet potato, peeled, chopped

1 lb potatoes, peeled chopped

1 medium onions, chopped

4 cups chicken broth

5 tbsp olive oil

2 cloves garlic, minced

1 red chili pepper, finely chopped

salt and pepper, to taste

½ cup heavy cream

Directions:

Heat the olive oil in a large pot over medium heat and sauté the onions, garlic and chili pepper until just fragrant. Add the potatoes and sweet potatoes and add in the chicken broth. Bring to a boil.

Reduce heat to low and simmer 30 minutes or until potatoes are tender. Transfer the soup to a blender or food processor and blend, until smooth.

Return to the pot and continue cooking for a few more minutes. Remove soup from heat; stir in the cream.

Irish Carrot Soup

Serves 5-6

Ingredients:

5-6 carrots, peeled, chopped

2 potatoes, peeled, chopped

1 small onion, chopped

4 cups chicken broth

3 tbsp olive oil

salt and pepper, to taste

1 cup sour cream, to serve

Directions:

Heat olive oil in a deep saucepan over medium-high heat and sauté the onion and carrot until tender. Add in potatoes and chicken broth.

Bring to the boil then reduce heat and simmer, partially covered, for 30 minutes, or until carrots are tender.

Set aside to cool then blend in batches until smooth. Return soup to saucepan and cook, stirring, for 4-5 minutes, or until heated through. Season with salt and pepper and serve with a dollop of cream.

Spicy Carrot Soup

Serves 6-7

Ingredients:

10 carrots, peeled and chopped

2 medium onions, chopped

4-5 cups water

5 tbsp olive oil

2 cloves garlic, minced

1 big red chili pepper, finely chopped

½ bunch, fresh coriander, finely cut

salt and pepper to taste

½ cup heavy cream

Directions:

Heat the olive oil in a large pot over medium heat and sauté the onions, carrots, garlic and chili pepper until tender. Add 4-5 cups of water and bring to a boil.

Reduce heat to low and simmer 30 minutes. Transfer the soup to a blender or food processor and blend, until smooth. Return to the pot and continue cooking for a few more minutes.

Remove soup from heat; stir in the cream. Serve with coriander sprinkled over each serving.

Main Dishes

Chicken with Almonds and Prunes

Serves 4

Ingredients:

1.5 lb chicken thigh fillets, trimmed

1/2 cup fresh orange juice

2 tbsp honey

1/3 cup white wine

1/2 cup pitted prunes

2 tbsp blanched almonds

2 tbsp raisins or sultanas

1 tsp ground cinnamon

salt and ground black pepper

1 tbsp fresh parsley leaves, chopped

couscous (to serve)

Directions:

Rinse chicken fillets and pat dry. Heat olive oil in a large skillet on medium heat. Working in batches cook the chicken pieces until nicely browned, 3-4 minutes each side. Transfer chicken to an ovenproof dish and set aside.

Combine orange juice, wine, honey, prunes, almonds, raisins and cinnamon in the same skillet. Bring to a boil, reduce heat to medium and boil for 5-8 minutes or until liquid is reduced by 1/3.

Pour over the chicken fillets and bake for 30 minutes, or until chicken is just tender. Season to taste with salt and pepper. Serve sprinkled with parsley and accompanied by couscous or orzo.

Sweet and Sour Sicilian Chicken

Serves 4

Ingredients:

4 chicken thigh fillets

1 large red onion, sliced

3 garlic cloves, chopped

2 tbsp flour

1/3 cup dry white wine

1 cup chicken broth

1/2 cup green olives

2 tbsp olive oil

2 bay leaves

1 tbsp fresh oregano leaves

2 tbsp brown sugar or honey

2 tbsp red wine vinegar

salt and black pepper, to taste

Directions:

Combine the flour with salt and black pepper and coat well all chicken pieces. Heat oil in ovenproof casserole and cook the chicken in batches, for 1-2 minutes each side, or until golden.

Add in onion, garlic, and wine and cook, stirring for 1 more minute. Add the chicken broth, olives, bay leaves, oregano, sugar and vinegar and bake, in a preheated to 380 F oven, for 20 minutes, or until the chicken is cooked through.

Carribean Chicken

Serves 4

Ingredients:

4-5 chicken breast halves

1 small red onion, finely cut

1 cup pineapple chunks

1 cup pineapple juice

1 tsp lime zest

1 tbsp soy sauce

1/2 tsp grated ginger

1/2 cup golden raisins

Directions:

Spray the slow cooker with non stick spray.

Dump all ingredients into slow cooker and turn chicken to coat.

Cook on low for 5-6 hours.

Mexican Lime Chicken

Serves 4

Ingredients:

4-5 chicken breast halves

2 garlic cloves, crushed

1 red pepper, thinly sliced

1/2 can sweet corn

1/4 cup lime juice

1/2 tsp lime zest

½ crushed coriander seeds

½ tsp hot paprika

1 tsp black pepper

1/4 tsp salt

Directions:

Preheat the oven to 350 F. Spray a casserole with non stick spray.

Place all ingredients into the casserole and turn chicken to coat.

Bake for about 40 minutes or until chicken juices run clear.

Peanut Butter Dump Chicken

Serves 4

Ingredients:

4-5 chicken breast halves, cut in 1 inch pieces

3-4 green onions, finely cut

4-5 white button mushrooms, sliced

¾ cup smooth peanut butter

1 tbsp soy sauce

Directions:

Preheat oven to 350 F.

Spray a casserole with non stick spray.

Place all ingredients into the casserole and turn chicken to coat.

Bake for about 40 minutes or until chicken juices run clear.

Blue Cheese and Mushroom Dump Chicken

Serves 4

Ingredients:

4 chicken breast halves

6-7 white button mushrooms, sliced

1 cup crumbled blue cheese

1/2 cup sour cream

salt and black pepper, to taste

1 cup walnuts, crushed, to serve

Directions:

Heat oven to 350 degrees F. Spray a casserole with non stick spray. Place all ingredients into it, turn chicken to coat.

Bake for 35-40 minutes or until chicken juices run clear. Sprinkle with walnuts and serve.

Pesto Chicken

Serves 4

Ingredients:

5-6 chicken breast halves

1 small jar pesto sauce

1 cup sour cream

Directions:

In a bowl, combine pesto and sour cream.

Heat oven to 350 degrees F. Spray a casserole with non stick spray. Place chicken and pesto mixture into it, turn chicken to coat.

Bake for 35-40 minutes or until chicken juices run clear.

Greek Chicken And Lemon Rice

Serves 4

Ingredients:

4 chicken thighs, skin on, bone in

1 small onion, finely cut

1 garlic clove, minced

1 cup white rice

1 1/2 cups water

3 tbsp olive oil

1 tsp salt

black pepper, to taste

for the marinade:

2 lemons, juiced

2 tbsp lemon zest

1 tbsp dried oregano

4 garlic cloves, minced

1 tsp salt

Directions:

Combine the chicken and marinade ingredients in a bowl and set aside for at least 30 minutes.

Heat olive oil in an ovenproof casserole dish on medium-high heat. Remove chicken from marinade, but reserve the marinade. Cook chicken pieces for a few minutes on each side, enough to seal them.

Add in onions, garlic, rice and reserved marinade and stir to combine.

Stir in water, season with salt and pepper to taste, and bake in a preheated to 350 F oven for 30-35 minutes or until the rice and chicken are done.

Spicy Chicken and Bean Stew

Serves 4

Ingredients:

4 chicken thighs, skin on, bone in

1 small onion, finely cut

1 garlic clove, minced

2 red chillies, deseeded and chopped

1 can tomatoes, diced and undrained

2 cans kidney beans, drained

1 cup hot chicken broth

3 tbsp olive oil

1 tsp hot paprika

1 tsp salt

black pepper, to taste

1/2 cup fresh parsley, finely cut, to serve

1 cup sour cream

Directions:

Heat the olive oil in an ovenproof casserole dish on medium-high heat. Cook chicken for a few minutes on each side, until brown all over.

Add in onions, garlic, chillies and hot paprika and stir to combine.

Stir in chicken broth, beans and tomatoes, season with salt and pepper to taste, cover, and cook until the chicken is cooked through and tender.

Stir through the parsley and serve with sour cream.

Mediterranean Chicken Stew

Serves 4

Ingredients:

4 chicken breast halves

1 large onion, sliced

1 red bell pepper, thinly sliced

2 cups tomato pasta sauce

1/2 cup black olives, pitted

1/2 green olives, pitted

1/3 cup Parmesan cheese

¼ cup chopped parsley

Directions:

Spray the slow cooker with non stick spray.

Combine all ingredients into slow cooker and turn chicken to coat. Cook on low for 7-8 hours.

Sprinkle with Parmesan cheese, parsley and serve.

Slow Cooker Herb Chicken and Vegetables

Serves 4

Ingredients:

4 skinless, boneless chicken breast halves

12 oz baby potatoes

1 onion, sliced

2 carrots, cut

1 red bell pepper, halved, deseeded, cut

1 zucchini, peeled and cut

4 garlic cloves, thinly sliced

1 cup chicken broth

1 tsp dry oregano

1 tsp dried rosemary

salt and pepper, to taste

Directions:

Spray the slow cooker with non stick spray.

Place vegetables in slow cooker. Season with a bit of salt and pepper.

Season chicken breasts with oregano and rosemary and place on top of vegetables.

Pour chicken broth over the chicken and vegetables. Cover and cook on low for about 6-7 hours.

Chicken With Spinach and Mushrooms

Serves 4

Ingredients:

4-5 skinless, boneless chicken breast halves

1 onion, chopped

1 lb button mushrooms, halved

1 red bell pepper, chopped

2-3 cloves garlic, minced

4-5 cups spinach, chopped

1/2 cup white wine

1/2 tsp rosemary

salt and black pepper, to taste

Directions:

Heat olive oil in an ovenproof casserole dish and brown the chicken. Add in onion, garlic, pepper, mushrooms and rosemary and sauté for 2-3 minutes, stirring.

Add in wine, season with salt and pepper to taste, and simmer for 10 minutes or until the wine is nearly evaporated.

Add in spinach, leave to wilt for 2 minutes, then stir through and serve.

Lemon-spiced Chicken with Chickpeas

Serves 5-6

Ingredients:

4-5 skinless, boneless chicken breast halves, cut into chunks

1 large onion, chopped

1 can chickpeas, drained

1 cup chicken broth

2 cups chopped spinach

2-3 cloves garlic, minced

juice from 1 lemon

1 tbsp lemon zest

1 tsp ground coriander

1 tsp ground cumin

1/2 tsp cinnamon

salt and black pepper, to taste

Directions:

Heat olive oil in an ovenproof casserole dish and brown the chicken. Add in onion, garlic, spices and lemon zest and sauté for a minute, stirring.

Add in chickpeas and broth, season with salt and pepper to taste, cover, and simmer for 10 minutes.

Add in spinach and re-cover. Leave to wilt for 2 minutes, then stir through. Squeeze over the lemon juice just before serving.

Honey Mustard Chicken with Parsnips

Serves 5-6

Ingredients:

7-8 chicken tights

1 onion, chopped

1 lb parsnips, peeled and cut into sticks

1 cup chicken broth

2 tbsp mustard

1 tbsp honey

1 tsp thyme

1/2 tsp cinnamon

salt and black pepper, to taste

Directions:

In a bowl, combine chicken broth, mustard and honey.

Heat olive oil in an ovenproof casserole dish and brown the chicken. Add in onion, and parsnips and sauté for a minute, stirring.

Stir in broth mixture, thyme and cinnamon, season with salt and pepper to taste, cover, and simmer for 30 minutes.

Andalusian Style Chicken

Serves 4-5

Ingredients:

2 large chicken breasts, cut into bite-sized pieces

1 medium onion, thinly sliced

1 red bell pepper, cut

2 garlic cloves, thinly sliced

1 cup cherry tomatoes, halved

1 cup hot chicken broth

a large pinch of saffron

a large pinch of cinnamon

1 red chilli, deseeded and chopped

2 tbsp sherry vinegar

1 tbsp honey

2 tbsp raisins

3 tbsp toasted pine nuts or almonds

salt and black pepper, to taste

1/2 cup parsley leaves, finely cut, to serve

Directions:

Add the saffron to the hot chicken broth to soak.

In a deep saucepan, heat the oil over medium heat and cook the onion until it is soft and golden.

Push to the side of the pan and add the chicken. Cook for a few minutes until the chicken is browned all over.

Add the cinnamon and chilli, and cook for a couple of minutes. Add in the broth, vinegar, honey, tomatoes and raisins.

Bring to the boil, lower the heat and simmer for 15 mins until has thickened and the chicken is cooked through.

Sprinkle with coriander and nuts, and serve.

Portuguese Style Chicken

Serves 4

Ingredients:

1 whole chicken

4 garlic cloves, crushed

1/3 cup lime juice

3 tbsp olive oil

1 tbsp chilli flakes

1 tsp ground coriander

1 tbsp paprika

1 tsp dried oregano

1 tsp salt

Directions:

Using a sharp knife, cut through bones on either side of backbone. Remove backbone, place chicken breast side up into a bowl.

Combine lime juice, olive oil, garlic, chilli, salt, coriander, paprika and oregano together in a cup. Pour over chicken, cover, and refrigerate for at least two hours.

In a slow cooker, add the chicken and pour excess marinade juices over the top. Cook on low for 6-7 hours. Serve with vegetable salad or boiled potatoes.

Slow Cooked Chicken with Tomatoes and Artichokes

Serves 4

Ingredients:

3 skinless chicken breasts, cut into strips

2 leeks, white parts only, chopped

1 can quartered artichokes, drained

1 can diced tomatoes

1/2 green olives, halved

2 garlic cloves, crushed

1 tsp lemon rind

7-8 fresh basil leaves, chopped

1 bay leaf

salt and pepper, to taste

1 cup finely cut parsley

Directions:

Spray the slow cooker with non stick spray.

Combine all ingredients into slow cooker and turn chicken to coat. Cook on low for 7-8 hours. Remove bay leave and serve sprinkled with parsley.

Homemade Lasagna

Serves 9-10

Ingredients:

1.5 lbs lean ground beef

10 oz pancetta or bacon, cut into 1/4-inch pieces

1 onion, finely chopped

2 carrots, chopped

2 celery ribs, chopped

3 garlic cloves, crushed

1/2 cup dry white wine

1/2 cup chicken broth

2 cups canned tomatoes, diced

3 tbsp tomato paste

1 tbsp dried basil

1/3 cup parsley

1/2 tsp ground black pepper

1/4 tsp salt

1 tsp paprika

2 cups mozzarella cheese, shredded

1 cup Parmesan cheese, shredded

12 no-boil lasagna noodles

Directions:

Heat olive oil in a large pot and cook ground beef, pancetta, onion, carrots, celery, and garlic over medium-high heat until ground meat turns brown. Bring to a simmer and cook, uncovered, until liquid is nearly evaporated. Stir in wine and beef broth and continue simmering until liquid evaporates. Add in paprika, tomatoes, tomato paste, parsley, black pepper and salt.

Combine mozzarella and Parmesan cheese in a medium bowl.

Spread one-third of the meat sauce over the bottom of an ungreased 13x9x2-inch baking dish. Cover with one-fourth of the cheese mixture. Layer noodles. Repeat layering meat sauce, cheese mixture, and noodles two more times.

Cover dish with foil and bake in a preheated to 350 F oven for 40 minutes. Sprinkle with remaining cheese mixture and bake, uncovered, about 5 more minutes until the cheese turns gold. Set aside for 10 minutes and serve.

Beef and Spinach Lasagna

Serves 8-10

Ingredients:

1 lb lean ground beef

10 oz frozen spinach

1 onion, chopped

2 cups canned tomatoes

4 garlic cloves, crushed

1 tsp dried basil

1 tsp dried oregano

2 cups ricotta cheese

2 cups mozzarella cheese, shredded

12 no-cook lasagna noodles

Directions:

In a large skillet, sauté onion for a few minutes. Add beef and cook over medium heat until meat is no longer pink. Add in the tomatoes, garlic, basil and oregano. Simmer for 10 minutes. In a large bowl, combine the thawed spinach with half the ricotta and mozzarella cheese.

Spread one-third of the meat sauce over the bottom of an ungreased 13x9x2-inch baking dish. Sprinkle with one-fourth of the spinach -cheese mixture. Top with noodles. Repeat layering meat sauce, spinach mixture, and noodles two more times.

Cover dish with foil. Bake for 40 minutes in a preheated to 350 F oven. Sprinkle with the remaining cheese mixture. Bake, uncovered, about 5 minutes until cheese turns golden. Let stand for at least 10 minutes before serving.

Mediterranean Bolognaise

Serves 6

Ingredients:

1.5 lbs ground lean beef

1 onion, chopped

2 garlic cloves, finely chopped

2 tbsp tomato paste

2 cups canned tomatoes, diced, undrained

1/3 cup dried tomatoes, chopped

1/4 cup black olives, pitted, halved

1/4 cup chopped fresh basil leaves

1 tsp dried oregano

17 oz spaghetti

Parmesan cheese, to serve

Directions:

Heat oil in a large saucepan over medium-high heat. Add ground beef, onion and garlic.

Cook, stirring, for 7-8 minutes, or until the meat has browned. Add tomato paste, tomatoes, dried tomatoes, olives, basil and oregano and continue cooking, for 6 minutes, or until thickened. Season with salt and pepper.

Prepare spaghetti as described on package directions. Wash, drain and divide them between bowls. Top with sauce and sprinkle with Parmesan cheese and fresh basil leaves.

Ground Beef Pasta with Yogurt Sauce

Serves 5

Ingredients:

2 cups small pasta

1 lb ground beef

1 onion, chopped

2 tbsp butter

2 tbsp olive oil

salt and black pepper, to taste

for the sauce:

1 1/2 cup yogurt, room temperature

5 garlic cloves, crushed

Directions:

Prepare the sauce by mixing well yogurt and garlic.

Sauté the onion in olive oil, for 2-3 minutes over medium heat. Add the ground beef and cook for 10 minutes, or until the meat is cooked through.

Cook pasta as described on package instructions. Drain and set aside. Melt the butter in a large pot and toss the pasta in it.

Serve pasta, topped with the cooked ground beef and generously covered with the yogurt sauce.

Baked Ground Beef Pasta

Serves 6

Ingredients:

2 cups large pasta

1 lb ground beef

2 onions, finely chopped

4 garlic cloves, chopped

3-4 mushrooms, chopped

5-6 pickled gherkins, chopped

1 cup canned tomatoes, drained

1 tsp paprika

1 tsp dry basil

salt and black pepper, to taste

1/2 cup parsley leaves, chopped

1 cup mozzarella cheese, grated

1 egg, whisked

Directions:

Prepare pasta according to package directions. Drain and place in an oven proof dish.

Heat olive oil in a large pot and sauté onion until transparent. Add ground beef, mushrooms, garlic and tomatoes, stir and cook on low heat for about 15 minutes. When the meat is almost done, add the gherkins, the parsley and toss everything with the pasta. Whisk the egg with mozzarella cheese and spread all over the pasta equally. Bake in a preheated to 350 F oven for 10 minutes or until the cheese turns golden.

Beef Stew with Green Peas

Serves 6

Ingredients:

2 lbs stewing beef

2 bags(10 oz each) frozen peas

1 onion, diced

3-4 garlic cloves, cut

2 carrots, chopped

1/3 cups olive oil

1 cup water

1 tsp salt

1 tbsp paprika

1/2 cup fresh dill, finely chopped

1 cup yogurt (optional)

Directions:

Season the meat pieces with salt and black pepper. Heat the olive oil in a large stewing pot and sauté the onion and meat until the meat is well browned. Add in paprika, carrots, garlic, frozen peas and water.

Bring to the boil, then reduce heat, cover, and simmer for an hour. Serve sprinkled with fresh dill and a dollop of yogurt.

Potato Beef Stew

Serves 6

Ingredients:

2 lbs stewing beef

5 potatoes, cubed

2 carrots, chopped

1 onion, sliced

3 garlic cloves, crushed

4 tbsp tomato paste or purée

1 cup water

3 tbsp olive oil

1 tsp paprika

1/2 tsp summer savory

1 tsp salt

½ tsp ground black pepper

Directions:

Heat olive oil in a large soup pot over medium-high heat and sauté the beef pieces for 3-4 minutes until well sealed. Add carrots, onion and garlic and sauté for 3 more minutes, stirring. Add paprika and summer savory and stir.

Dissolve the tomato paste in a cup of water and pour over the meat. Add salt and black pepper and stir again. Bring to the boil, then reduce heat and simmer for 40 minutes.

Add potatoes and simmer for 20 more minutes, or until potatoes are tender. Sprinkle with chopped parsley and serve hot.

Beef with Mushrooms

Serves 4

Ingredients:

1 lb stewing beef

2 cups mushrooms, sliced

2 leeks, chopped

4 garlic cloves, sliced

3 tbsp olive oil

2 tbsp tomato paste or purée

1/2 cup water

1/2 cup dry red wine

1 tsp paprika

1 tsp dried thyme

1 tsp salt

1 tsp sugar

black pepper, to taste

Directions:

Heat the olive oil in a large pot and seal the beef pieces very well. Add in the leeks, garlic and white wine, and cook over low heat until the beef pieces are tender.

Add sugar, paprika, thyme, salt and pepper and stir. Dilute the tomato paste in half a cup of hot water. Pour it over the meat, stir, and add the mushrooms. Cover and simmer, stirring from time to time, over medium-low heat for 40 minutes.

Uncover and simmer some more until the liquid has evaporated.

Beef and Spinach Stew

Serves 6

Ingredients:

1 lb stewing beef

10 oz frozen spinach or 6 cups fresh spinach leaves, cut

1 onion, chopped

1 carrot, chopped

1 cup mushrooms, cut

3 garlic cloves, crushed

1 cup beef broth

1/2 cup canned tomatoes, drained

4 tbsp olive oil

6 oz butter

1 tbsp paprika

salt and pepper, to taste

Directions:

In a large stew pot, heat the butter and olive oil and seal the beef pieces. Add onion, carrot, mushrooms and garlic and sauté for a few minutes. Add paprika, beef broth and bring to the boil t hen reduce heat and simmer, covered, for 30-40 minutes.

Add tomatoes and spinach. Stir and simmer, uncovered, for 10 minutes. Serve over rice or couscous.

Beef and Okra Stew

Serves 6

Ingredients:

1 lb stewing beef

1 lb frozen okra

1 onion, chopped

3 garlic cloves, crushed

1 cup canned tomatoes, diced

3 tbsp tomato purée

1/2 tsp cumin

1 tsp coriander

1 cup water

4 tbsp olive oil

salt and pepper, to taste

Directions:

In a large saucepan, heat olive oil and seal meat. Add onions and garlic and sauté, stirring for 2-3 minutes. Add tomatoes, cumin, coriander, salt and pepper. Add water and tomato purée.

Stir and combine well. Add okra and bring to a boil, then reduce heat to low and simmer, covered, for an hour or until meat is tender and done. Uncover and simmer for five more minutes. Serve with white rice or couscous.

Mixed Vegetables with Beef

Serves 6-8

Ingredients:

2 lbs stewing beef

2 eggplants, peeled and cubed

5 small potatoes, peeled and halved

1 zucchini, peeled and cubed

2 red peppers, cut

1 cup frozen okra

1 onion, sliced

4 garlic cloves, cut

3 tomatoes, diced

1 cup parsley leaves, chopped

1/4 cup olive oil

1 tsp paprika

salt and black pepper, to taste

Directions:

Sprinkle the eggplant pieces with salt and set aside in a strainer for 15 minutes. Wash the salt and the excess juices and pat dry the eggplant pieces.

Heat the olive oil in a large pot and sauté the beef pieces for a few minutes until well browned. Add in the vegetables, stirring. Add paprika, salt and pepper and stir very well.

Transfer the meat and vegetables to an ovenproof dish and bake in a preheated oven for 30 min. Sprinkle with parsley and serve.

Stuffed Tomatoes with Bulgur and Ground Beef

Serves 6

Ingredients:

1 lb ground beef

6 large tomatoes

2 tbsp tomato paste or purée

1/2 cup bulgur

1 onion, shredded

2 garlic cloves, crushed

6 tsp sugar

1 tsp paprika

1 tsp mint

1/2 cup parsley leaves, finely cut

5 tbsp olive oil

salt and pepper to taste

2/3 cup Parmesan cheese, grated

Directions:

Slice the tops of the tomatoes in such a way as to be able to stuff the tomato and cover with the cap. With the help of a spoon, scoop out the tomato flesh and reserve in a bowl. Sprinkle a tsp of sugar in each tomato to help reduce the acidity.

Heat the olive oil in a large skillet and brown the ground beef. Add the onions and garlic and cook until transparent. Add the bulgur, parsley, finely cut tomato pulp and tomato paste. Season with paprika, mint, salt and pepper.

Bring to the boil, then reduce heat and simmer for 5 minutes.

Drizzle some olive oil in the bottom of an oven proof dish. Arrange the tomatoes in the dish. Stuff them with the meat mixture - each tomato should be about 3/4 full.

Sprinkle with Parmesan cheese and bake in a preheated to 350 F oven for 30 minutes.

Stuffed Artichokes

Serves 6

Ingredients:

1 lb lean ground beef

1/3 cup rice, washed and drained

6 large firm fresh artichokes

1 onion, grated

2 garlic cloves, chopped

4 tomatoes, grated

5 tbsp olive oil

1/2 cup parsley leaves, very finely cut

1 tsp paprika

salt and pepper, to taste

juice of 1/2 lemon

Directions:

Peel artichokes and cut off tips. With the help of a spoon, carve out the center of artichokes. Put them in a large bowl together with a tbsp of salt, lemon juice and enough water to cover them completely.

Heat olive oil in a cooking pot and sauté onions and garlic until transparent. Add in ground beef, rice, parsley and paprika. Cook for 5 min, stirring. Add tomatoes and cook until almost all liquid evaporates. Season with salt and pepper and remove from heat.

Wash and drain artichokes. Stuff each with the meat mixture and arrange them in a cooking pot. Add 2 cups of water and bring to the boil, then reduce heat and simmer for about 40 minutes.

Stuffed Cabbage Leaves with Ground Beef and Rice

Serves 8

Ingredients:

1 lb ground beef

20-30 medium sized pickled cabbage leaves

1 onion, diced

1 leek, finely cut

1/2 cup white rice

2 tsp tomato paste

2 tsp paprika

1 tsp dried mint

½ tsp black pepper

1/3 cup olive oil

salt to taste

Directions:

Sauté the onion and leek in the oil for about 2-3 minutes. Remove from heat and add the beef, tomato paste, paprika, mint, black pepper and the washed and drained rice. Add salt only if the cabbage leaves are not too salty. Mix everything very well.

In a large pot place a few cabbage leaves on the base. Place a cabbage leaf on a large plate with the thickest part closest to you. Spoon 1-2 teaspoons of the meat mixture and fold over each edge to create a tight sausage-like parcel.

Place in the pot in two or three layers. Cover with a few cabbage leaves and pour over some boiling water so that the water level remains lower than the top layer of cabbage leaves. Top with a small dish upside down to prevent scattering. Bring to the boil, then lower the heat and cook for around an hour.

Meatballs with Parsley Sauce

Serves 6-8

Ingredients:

2 lbs lean ground beef

4 slices bacon, finely cut

1 onion, finely chopped

2 garlic cloves, finely chopped

1/2 cup parsley leaves, very finely cut

1/2 cup breadcrumbs, for coating

1 cup olive oil for frying

for the sauce:

1 cup breadcrumbs

3 cups beef broth

1 cup parsley leaves, finely cut

1/4 cup walnuts, crushed

Directions:

Place the ground beef, onion, garlic, parsley and bacon in a large bowl and mix with hands. Form into meatballs.

Heat olive oil in a large frying pan. Put the breadcrumbs on a plate and coat each meatball. Fry meatballs in the frying pan in batches, turning, until the meat is cooked through. When ready place them on a paper towel to absorb the extra oil.

Put the broth, breadcrumbs and a cup of parsley leaves into a large pot. Stir and bring to a boil. Add the nuts and stir. Simmer for about 5 minutes. Add the meatballs to the parsley sauce. Serve over rice or with potato mash.

Meatballs with Egg-lemon Sauce

Serves 4

Ingredients:

1 lb ground beef

1 large egg

1/3 cup all-purpose flour

1/3 cup white rice, washed and drained

1 onion, shredded

2 garlic cloves, crushed

2 tsp dried parsley

1 tsp dried mint

salt and black pepper, to taste

3 cups beef or chicken broth

for the sauce:

3 eggs yolks

Juice of three large lemons

Directions:

Combine beef, rice, egg, onion, garlic, parsley, mint, salt, and black pepper in a mixing bowl. Mix well with hands and roll tablespoonfuls of the mixture into balls. Put flour in a small bowl and roll each meatball in the flour, coating entire surface, then set aside on a large plate.

Heat two cups of beef broth in a large pot until boiling and add the meatballs. The broth should be enough to cover them. Bring to the boil, then reduce heat and simmer, covered, for 30-40 minutes. Add more broth if necessary.

Whisk egg yolks and lemon in a bowl. Take 1-2 ladles of broth from the pot with the meatballs. Mix it with the sauce, then pour it all back slowly into the pot. Cook for 10 more minutes.

Spinach with Ground Beef

Serves 4

Ingredients:

10 oz ground beef

6 cups fresh spinach, chopped

1 tomato, cubed

1 onion, finely chopped

1/3 cup rice

4 tbsp olive oil

1 tsp paprika

salt, to taste

black pepper, to taste

Directions:

Heat the olive oil in a large pot and sauté the onion for about 2-3 minutes. Add the ground beef, paprika, salt and black pepper and stir. Cook until the the ground beef turns brown.

Add in the rice, tomato cubes, and stir again. Simmer, covered, for 20 minutes.

Add the spinach and cook until it wilts. Serve with a dollop of yogurt.

Ground Beef and Chickpea Casserole

Serves 6

Ingredients:

1 lb ground beef

1 onion, chopped

2 garlic cloves, crushed

1 can chickpeas, drained

1 can sweet corn, drained

1 can tomato sauce

1/2 cup water

2 bay leaves

1 tsp dried oregano

1/2 tsp salt

1/2 tsp cumin

3 tbsp olive oil

black pepper, to taste

Directions:

Heat the olive oil in a casserole over medium-high heat. Add the onion and sauté for 4-5 minutes. Add garlic and sauté a minute more. Add in the ground beef and cook for 5 minutes, stirring, until browned. Add the cumin and bay leaves, the tomatoes, corn and chickpeas.

Bring everything to the boil, then reduce heat and simmer for 20 minutes, or until the beef is cooked through. Remove the bay leaves and serve over pilaf or couscous.

Greek Lamb Stew

Serves 4

Ingredients:

2 lbs cubed stewing lamb

1 onion, finely cut

1 carrot, chopped

2 garlic cloves, chopped

1 can tomatoes, diced and undrained

4 cups chicken broth

12 oz orzo, uncooked

1 tsp oregano

1 tsp ground cinnamon

3 tbsp olive oil

½ tsp black pepper and ½ tsp salt

freshly grated Parmesan, to serve

Directions:

Heat the oil in an ovenproof casserole dish.

Add the lamb, onions, oregano, ground cinnamon, salt and pepper, and stir well. Bake, uncovered, for 45 mins, stirring halfway.

add the tomatoes and broth, cover, and return to the oven for 1½ hrs, until the lamb is tender.

Stir in the orzo. Cover again, and cook for a further 20 mins, stirring halfway through. Sprinkle with grated Parmesan and serve.

Hearty Lamb Stew

Serves 4

Ingredients:

1 lb cubed stewing lamb

1 onion, thinly sliced

3 carrots, chopped

2 garlic cloves, chopped

3 leeks, chopped

1 can cannellini beans, drained

1 1/2 cup chicken broth

1 tsp dried rosemary

a pinch of saffron

3 tbsp olive oil

½ tsp black pepper

½ tsp salt

Directions:

Heat the oil in an ovenproof casserole dish.

Brown the lamb in the oil for 5-6 minutes, or until golden all over. Add in the onion, garlic, carrots, leeks and all other ingredients. Stir to coat.

Cover with a lid and cook over low heat for 1 hour.

Sweet Spiced Lamb Shanks With Quince

Serves 4

Ingredients:

4 trimmed lamb shanks

1 onion, thinly sliced

2 garlic cloves, chopped

2 quince, peeled and quartered

1 tbsp tomato paste

1 tbsp honey

1 1/2 cup chicken broth

juice of one lemon

1 tbsp lemon zest

2 tsp ground cinnamon

2 tsp ground coriander

1 tsp ground ginger

1 tsp ground cumin

a pinch of saffron

3 tbsp olive oil

½ tsp black pepper

½ tsp salt

Directions:

Heat the oil in an ovenproof casserole dish.

Season the shanks, then brown in the oil for 5-6 minutes, or until golden all over. Add in the onion, garlic, the quartered quince and all other ingredients. Stir to coat.

Cover with a lid and braise in the oven for 2 hours.

Slow Cooked Lamb with Red Wine Sauce

Serves 4

Ingredients:

4 trimmed lamb shanks

1 onion, thinly sliced

2 large carrots, roughly chopped

2-3 parsnips, roughly chopped

1 cup chicken broth

2 cups dry red wine

1 tsp brown sugar

½ tsp black pepper

½ tsp salt

Directions:

Spray the slow cooker with non stick spray.

Place the lamb shanks in it together with all other ingredients.

Cover and cook on low for 6-7 hours.

Slow Cooked Mediterranean Lamb

Serves 4

Ingredients:

1 1/2 lb boneless leg of lamb, trimmed and cubed

1 onion, thinly sliced

2 large carrots, roughly chopped

2 garlic cloves, chopped

1 cup chicken broth

1 can chickpeas, drained

1 cup raisins

1/2 cup dried figs, halved

4 tbsp fresh mint, finely cut

1/4 tsp saffron threads, crushed

1 tsp ground ginger

½ tsp black pepper

½ tsp salt

3 tbsp olive oil

Directions:

Heat oil in a large non stick frying pan and cook the lamb in batches, for 3-4 minutes each side, or until golden. Transfer to slow cooker.

Add in all other ingredients. Cover and cook on low for 7-9 hours.

Slow Cooked Lamb with Lemon, Dill and Feta

Serves 4

Ingredients:

4 lamb shanks

1 small onion, thinly sliced

2 garlic cloves, chopped

1 cup chicken broth

1/2 cup fresh dill, finely cut

1 medium lemon, thinly sliced

1 cup crumbled feta cheese

2 tbsp olive oil

½ tsp black pepper

½ tsp salt

3 tbsp olive oil

Directions:

Season the lamb shanks with salt and pepper. Heat oil in a large non stick frying pan and cook the lamb in batches, for 3-4 minutes each side, or until golden. Transfer to slow cooker.

Add the chicken broth, 2 tablespoons of dill, garlic, onion and lemon slices. Cover and cook on low until the lamb is tender, about 8-9 hours.

Sprinkle with the feta and the remaining dill and serve with orzo or rice.

Slow Cooked Beef Couscous

Serves 5-6

Ingredients:

2 lbs stewing beef

1 large onion, cut

1/2 cup canned chickpeas, drained

2 carrots

1/2 cup green peas

1/2 cup black olives, pitted

3 tbsp tomato paste

2 cupc beef broth

1 zucchini, peeled and cut

1 cup frozen green beans

3 potatoes, peeled and cut

1 tsp cumin

1 tsp paprika

a small bunch of fresh parsley

Directions:

Place beef, onion, chickpeas, green peas, carrot, olives, tomato paste, cumin, paprika and beef broth in slow cooker. Tie the parsley into a bouquet and place it on top. Cover and cook on low for 10 hours.

Add green beans, potatoes and zucchini, season with salt and pepper to taste, increase heat setting to high and cook for 1 hour more. In the end discard the parsley bouquet.

Serve over cooked couscous with meat and vegetables on top and stew sauce in a separate bowl.

Beef and Root Vegetable Crock Pot

Serves 6

Ingredients:

2 lbs stewing beef

2 carrots, cut

2 onions, sliced

1 small turnip, peeled and diced

1 small beet, peeled and diced

1 cup beef broth

1 tsp tomato paste

1 tbsp paprika

2 bay leaves

1 cup yogurt, to serve

Directions:

Spray the crock pot with non stick spray.

Combine all ingredients in crockpot. Cover and cook on low for 6-9 hours.

One-pot Pork Chops With Fennel and Potatoes

Serves 4

Ingredients:

4-5 pork chops

2 potatoes, peeled and cut into wedges

1 fennel bulb, peeled and cut into wedges

1 red pepper, deseeded and cut into wedges

1/2 cup sun-dried tomatoes

3 tbsp olive oil

1 cup chicken broth

1 tsp thyme

salt and black pepper, to taste

Directions:

Put the potatoes, fennel, pepper, thyme and tomatoes in a large casserole. Stir in chicken broth, cover and bake in a preheated to 420 F oven for 30 minutes.

Place the pork chops between the vegetables in the casserole. Season with salt and black pepper to taste and return to the oven for 15-20 minutes or until the pork chops are golden and cooked through.

Pork Chops with Balsamic Roasted Vegetables

Serves 4

Ingredients:

4 pork chops

12 oz small red potatoes, halved

8 oz cremini mushrooms, halved

3-4 carrots, cut into sticks

1 medium red onion, cut into wedges

1 tsp thyme

1/2 tsp ground cumin

4 tbsp olive oil

1 tsp tomato paste

1/3 cup chicken broth

1 tbsp honey

3 tbsp balsamic vinegar

1/2 cup Gorgonzola cheese, crumbled

salt and black pepper, to taste

Directions:

Heat olive oil in an ovenproof casserole and cook pork chops 3 minutes on each side or until browned. Add the potatoes, carrots, onion and mushrooms. Season with salt and pepper, sprinkle with thyme and cumin.

In a bowl, combine tomato paste, balsamic vinegar, honey and chicken broth. Pour this mixture over the pork chops and vegetables. Cover and bake in a preheated to 420 F on for 30 minutes, stirring halfway through.

Juicy Pork Chops

Serves 4

Ingredients:

4-5 pork chops, about 4 oz each

4 garlic cloves, crushed

1 tbsp honey

3 tbsp olive oil

1 tbsp vinegar

1/2 cup white wine

1 tbsp soy sauce

1 tbsp ketchup

1/2 tsp dried sage

1 tsp black pepper

1/2 tsp salt

Directions:

In a cup, combine all liquid ingredients and stir until very well mixed. Crush the garlic, sage, black pepper and salt together into a paste. R

ub each chop with the garlic paste and arrange them in a casserole dish.

Pour the liquid mix over the chops. Cover the casserole and bake in a preheated to 350 F on for 45 minutes, or until the chops are cooked through.

One-pot Pork with Orange and Olives

Serves 4

Ingredients:

2 lbs pork shoulder, cut into cubes

2 lbs potatoes, peeled and cut into large wedges

2 onions, chopped

4-5 garlic cloves, chopped

1 can tomatoes, undrained

1/2 cup sun-dried tomatoes

1 cup black olives, halved

3 bay leaves

3 tbsp olive oil

1/2 cup orange juice

1/2 cup white wine

1 tsp paprika

1 tsp orange zest

salt and black pepper, to taste

Directions:

Heat olive in an ovenproof casserole and seal pork until golden. Stir in onions, garlic, paprika, orange zest, wine and orange juice. Add potatoes, bay leaves, olives, sun-dried tomatoes and canned tomatoes. Stir to combine.

Cover the casserole and bake in a preheated to 350 F on for 45 minutes, or until the chops are cooked through. Uncover and cook until the liquid evaporates.

Mediterranean Pork Casserole

Serves 4

Ingredients:

1 1/2lb pork loin, cut into cubes

1 large onion, chopped

1 cup mushrooms, cut

½ cup chicken broth

2 garlic cloves, finely chopped

1 green pepper, deseeded and cut into strips

1 red pepper, deseeded and cut into strips

1 tomato, chopped

2 tsp olive oil

1 tsp savory

1 tsp paprika

salt and black pepper, to taste

Directions:

Add the olive oil to a casserole dish and seal the pork cubes for about 5 minutes, stirring continuously. Lower the heat, add the onion and garlic and sauté for 3-4 minutes until the onion is soft.

Add the paprika and savory and season with salt and pepper to taste. Stir in the peppers, tomato, chicken broth and mushrooms. Cover with foil and bake for 1 hour at 350 F, or until the pork is tender. Uncover and bake for 5 minutes more. Serve with boiled potatoes.

Pork Roast and Cabbage

Serves 4

Ingredients:

2 cups cooked pork roast, chopped

1/2 head cabbage

1 onion, chopped

1 lemon, juice only

1 tomato, chopped

2 tbsp olive oil

1 tsp paprika

1/2 tsp cumin

black pepper, to taste

Directions:

In an ovenproof casserole dish, heat olive oil and gently sauté cabbage, pork and onions. Add in cumin, paprika, lemon juice, tomato and stir.

Cover, and bake at 350 F for 20-25 minutes, or until vegetables are tender.

Turkey Sausage and Lentil One-pot

Serves 4

Ingredients:

1 lb lean smoked turkey sausage, cut into 1-inch slices

1 big onion, chopped

2 garlic cloves, crushed

1 red pepper, sliced

1 cup green lentils, rinsed

1 cup vegetable broth

1 tbsp dried mint

1/2 cup finely cut parsley, to serve

Directions:

Place sausages, onions, garlic and red pepper in a pot. Add in lentils, vegetable broth and mint.

Stir, cover, and simmer for for 20 mins until lentils have softened and sausages are cooked through. Serve sprinkled with fresh parsley.

Sausage and Vegetable One-pot

Serves 4

Ingredients:

12 good-quality sausage, cut into 1 inch slices

1 big onion, chopped

1 fennel bulb, quartered, then sliced

1 red pepper, sliced

1 garlic clove, crushed

½ red chilli, finely chopped

1 pack green beans, halved

1 cup broad beans, double podded

1 cup peas

1 cup sour cream

1/2 cup vegetable broth

2 tbsp fresh basil

1/2 cup fresh parsley

salt and pepper, to taste

Directions:

Place the sausages, onions, garlic and red pepper in a pot. Add in the fennel and chilli. Cook for a few minutes, stirring, until browned all over. Add the vegetable broth, cover and simmer for 30 minutes.

Stir in beans and simmer for 4-5 minutes. Add the cream, basil and parsley, season with salt and pepper to taste, and serve.

Mediterranean Baked Fish

Serves 4

Ingredients:

1 ½ flounder or sole fillets

3 tomatoes, chopped

1/2 onion, chopped

2 cloves garlic, chopped

1/3 cup white wine

20 black olives, pitted and chopped

1 tbsp capers

3 tbsp olive oil

1 tbsp fresh lemon juice

1 tsp dry oregano

4 leaves fresh basil, chopped

3 tbsp Parmesan cheese

Directions:

Preheat oven to 350 F. Heat olive oil in an ovenproof casserole and sauté onion until translucent. Add in garlic, oregano and tomatoes. Stir and cook for 4-5 minutes.

Add wine, olives, capers, lemon juice and the chopped basil. Blend in Parmesan cheese, and arrange fish in this sauce. Bake for 20 minutes in the preheated oven, until fish is easily flaked with a fork.

Eggplant and Chickpea Stew

Serves: 4

Ingredients:

2-3 eggplants, peeled and diced

1 onion, chopped

2-3 garlic cloves, crushed

8 oz can chickpeas, drained

8 oz can tomatoes, undrained, diced

1 tbsp paprika

1/2 tsp cinnamon

1 tsp cumin

3 tbsp olive oil

salt and pepper, to taste

Directions:

Spray the slow cooker with non stick spray.

Heat olive oil in a large deep frying pan and sauté the onion and crushed garlic for 1-2 minutes, stirring. Add in paprika, cumin and cinnamon. Transfer to slow cooker.

Add in eggplant, tomatoes and chickpeas. Cover and cook on low for 6-7 hours or about 4 hours on high.

Eggplant Stew

Serves 4

Ingredients:

2 medium eggplants, peeled and diced

1 cup canned tomatoes, drained and diced

1 zucchini, diced

9-10 black olives, pitted

1 onion, chopped

4 garlic cloves, chopped

2 tbsp tomato paste

1 cup canned tomatoes, drained and diced

1 bunch of parsley, chopped, to serve

3 tbsp olive oil

½ tsp paprika

salt and black pepper, to taste

Directions:

Gently saute onions, garlic, and eggplants in olive oil on medium-high heat for 10 minutes. Add paprika and tomato paste and stir for 1-2 minutes.

Add in the rest of the ingredients. Cover and simmer on low-heat for 30 40 minutes. Sprinkle with parsley and serve.

Squash, Lentil and Bean One-pot

Serves: 4

Ingredients:

1 lb butternut squash, peeled, deseeded and diced

1 small onion, finely cut

1 can tomatoes, diced and undrained

2-3 garlic cloves, crushed

1/2 cup dry red lentil

1 can kidney beans

1 tbsp brown sugar

1 tsp paprika

1 tsp cumin

½ tsp chilli flakes

1 cup water

2 tsp red wine vinegar

2 tbsp olive oil

salt and pepper, to taste

1 cup fresh parsley, finely cut, to serve

Directions:

In a deep saucepan, heat olive oil and gently saute onion and squash for 5-8 mins until the onion is softened.

Add in spices and stir to combine. All all other ingredients except the parsley.

Stir to combine, cover, and cook on low heat for 35-40 minutes.

Sprinkle with parsley before serving.

Maple Roast Parsnip with Pear and Sage

Serves: 4

Ingredients:

6-7 small parsnips, peeled, halved

3-4 pears, cut into wedges

1-2 onions, cut into wedges

1 tsp garlic powder

1 tsp paprika

1 tsp dried oregano

1/2 cup fresh sage leaves

3 tbsp maple syrup

4 tbsp olive oil

Directions:

Preheat oven to 350F. Line 2 baking trays with baking paper. Place the parsnips, pears, onions, and sage on the trays.

Combine the maple syrup, olive oil, garlic powder, oregano and paprika in a bowl.

Pour the maple mixture evenly over the parsnips, pears and onions and gently toss to combine.

Bake, turning once, for 40 minutes or until the parsnip is golden and tender.

Balsamic Roasted Carrots and Baby Onions

Serves: 4

Ingredients:

2-3 bunches baby carrots, scrubbed

10-15 small onions, halved

4 tbsp honey

1 tsp rosemary

3-4 tbsp balsamic vinegar

2 tbsp olive oil

salt and pepper, to taste

Directions:

Preheat oven to 350F. Line a baking tray with baking paper.

Place the carrots, onions, rosemary and oil in a large bowl and toss to coat. Arrange carrots and onions, in a single layer, on the baking tray. Roast for 30 minutes or until tender.

In a bowl, combine honey and vinegar. Sprinkle over the vegetables and toss to coat. Roast for 25-30 minutes more or until vegetables are tender and caramelised. Season with salt and pepper to taste and serve.

Summer Pasta Bake

Serves 4

Ingredients:

1 small eggplant, cubed

2 zucchinis, cubed

1 red onion, sliced

3 cloves garlic, crushed

1 green pepper, chopped

3 tomatoes, diced

4 tablespoons olive oil

sea salt and freshly ground black pepper to taste

1 tsp dried oregano

1 cup uncooked penne pasta

½ cup feta cheese, crumbled

Directions:

Place eggplant slices on a tray and sprinkle with plenty of salt. Let sit for 30 minutes, then rinse with cold water.

Combine all vegetables in a large baking dish. Add in olive oil, salt, pepper and oregano. Toss to coat the vegetables well. Bake in a preheated to 350 F oven until the vegetables are very soft.

Boil the pasta according to package directions. Drain and toss with the baked vegetables. Add cheese and toss to combine again. Season to taste with salt and black pepper and serve.

Mediterranean Vegetable Casserole

Serves 4-5

Ingredients:

2 cups uncooked small pasta

1 small red onion, chopped

1/2 cup canned chickpeas, drained

1/2 cup oil-packed sun-dried tomatoes, drained and thinly sliced

1/2 cup green olives, pitted and halved

1 can (8 ounces) tomato sauce

1 cup crumbled feta cheese

1/2 cup sour cream

2 tbsp fresh basil leaves, chopped

1 tsp dried oregano

1/2 tsp dried thyme

salt and black pepper, to taste

Directions:

Cook pasta according to package directions. In a large bowl, combine all remaining ingredients.

Drain pasta and toss with vegetable mixture. Transfer to baking dish coated with cooking spray. Bake, uncovered, at 375 F for 30-35 minutes or until heated through.

Baked Mediterranean Casserole with Tofu and Feta Cheese

Serves 4-5

Ingredients:

2 lbs small new potatoes, washed and halved

1/2 cup feta cheese, crumbled

1 cup spicy tofu pieces

3 cloves garlic, crushed

2 cups cherry or grape tomatoes

3 tbsp rosemary, chopped or minced

3 tbsp olive oil

1/2 cup Parmesan cheese

salt and pepper to taste

Directions:

Preheat the oven to 350 F. Put the sliced potatoes, garlic, olive oil, rosemary, salt and pepper in an oven proof baking dish and mix them all together well so that the potatoes are well coated.

Place in the oven and bake for 20 minutes then stir and add the tomatoes, tofu and feta cheese. Sprinkle with Parmesan cheese and cook for 15 minutes more.

Okra and Tomato Casserole

Serves 4-5

Ingredients:

1 lb okra, stem ends trimmed

4 large tomatoes, cut into wedges

3 garlic cloves, chopped

3 tbsp olive oil

1 tsp salt

black pepper, to taste

Directions:

In a large casserole, mix together trimmed okra, sliced tomatoes, the olive oil and the chopped garlic.

Add salt and pepper and toss to combine. Bake in e preheated to 400 F oven for 45 minutes until the okra is tender.

Zucchinis with Chickpeas and Rice

Serves 4

Prep time: 30 min

Ingredients:

3 zucchinis, peeled and diced

1 bunch green onions, finely chopped

2 medium tomatoes, diced

1/2 can chickpeas, drained

1/2 cup rice

1/2 cup black olives, pitted and halved

2 cups water

5 tbsp sunflower oil

1 tsp salt

1 tsp paprika

1 tsp black pepper

1/2 cup fresh dill, finely cut

Directions:

Sauté the onions in olive oil and a little water for 1-2 minutes or until soft.

Transfer the onions in a baking dish and add in zucchinis, chickpeas, tomatoes, olives, rice, salt, paprika, black pepper and water. Stir to combine well.

Cover with a lid or aluminum foil and bake at 350 F for 20 minutes, or until the rice is done.

Sprinkle with dill and serve.

Zucchini Fritters

Serves 4

Ingredients:

5-6 zucchinis, grated

3 eggs

1/2 cup fresh dill, finely cut

1 tsp fresh mint, chopped

3 garlic cloves, crushed

5-6 spring onions, very finely chopped

1 cup feta cheese, crumbled

salt and black pepper, to taste

1 cup flour

1/2 cup sunflower oil, for frying

Directions:

Grate zucchinis and put them in a colander. Sprinkle with salt set aside to drain for 15 minutes. Squeeze and place in a bowl. Add all the other ingredients except for flour and the sunflower oil. Stir very well. Add in flour and mix again.

Heat the sunflower oil in a frying pan. Drop a few scoops of the zucchini mixture and fry them on medium heat, making sure they don't touch. Fry for 3-5 minutes, until golden brown. Serve with yogurt.

Spinach with Eggs

Serves 2

Ingredients:

1 lb spinach, fresh or frozen

1 onion, finely cut

4 eggs

3 tbsp olive oil

1/4 tsp cumin

1 tsp paprika

salt and pepper, to taste

Directions:

Heat olive oil on medium-low heat in a skillet. Gently sauté onion for 3-4 minutes. Add paprika and cumin and stir. Add spinach and sauté some more until it wilts.

Season with salt and black pepper to taste. Prepare 4 holes on the spinach bed for the eggs.

Break an egg into each hole. Cover and cook until eggs are cooked through. Serve with bread and a dollop of yogurt.

Breakfasts and Desserts

Sausage, Egg and Tomato Sandwiches

Serves: 4

Ingredients:

8 slices wholewheat bread

4 sausages, halved

4 oz sharp cheddar cheese, thinly sliced

4 large eggs

1 tomato, thinly sliced

2 tbsp butter

salt and pepper, to taste

Directions:

In a skillet, heat the butter. Add the sausages and cook over moderate heat, turning, until browned and cooked through, about 8 minutes. Transfer to a plate.

Fry the eggs in the skillet over moderate heat until slightly runny in the center, about 4 minutes. Season with salt and pepper.

Set each egg on a toast slice. Top with the cheese, sausages and tomato, and close the sandwiches.

Grilled Chicken and Mozarella Toast

Serves: 4

Ingredients:

4 slices crusty bread

2 cooked chicken breasts, sliced thinly

1 tomato, sliced

2 green onions, finely chopped

4 oz baby mozzarella

4-5 basil leaves, torn

2 tbsp olive oil

salt and black pepper, to taste

Directions:

Preheat oven with grill settings on medium heat.

Place bread onto a baking sheet and drizzle with olive oil. Place into the oven and grill until crisp.

Top each slice with some basil leaves, the chicken slices, tomatoes and mozzarella. Season with salt and pepper to taste, and grill for a further 3-5 minutes, or until the cheese has warmed through. Sprinkle with remaining basil leaves and serve.

Grilled Egg and Feta Toast

Serves: 4

Ingredients:

4 slices crusty bread

1 1/2 cups crumbled feta cheese

2 tbsp finely cut dill

2 eggs, whisked

1 tomato, sliced

2 tbsp olive oil

salt and black pepper, to taste

Directions:

Preheat oven with grill settings on medium heat.

In a bowl, add eggs, feta cheese and dill. Stir to combine very well.

Place bread on a baking sheet and drizzle with olive oil. Spoon 1/4 of the cheese mixture on each slice of bread.

Grill for 5-6 minutes, or until the cheese is golden. Top with tomatoes and serve.

Italian Beef Sandwiches

Serves: 4

Ingredients:

1 loaf soft Italian bread (12 -inch)

2 tbsp butter

2 tbsp basil pesto

4 oz quality roast beef, thinly sliced

8 slices provolone cheese

1 tomato, thinly sliced

2 red bell peppers, sliced

1 cup baby rocket leaves

salt, to taste

Directions:

Split the bread lengthwise, then pull out some of the bread from the inside. Spread butter on the bottom half.

Layer roast beef, cheese, tomato, pepper and rocket. Spread the cut side of the bread top with basil pesto then place on top of the sandwich.

Cut into 4 pieces and serve.

Sausage, Tomato and Cheese Sandwiches

Serves: 4

Ingredients:

4 sausages

1 tbsp butter

8 slices rye bread

1/4 cup cream cheese

2 cups sprouts

1 tomato, thinly sliced

4 slices cheddar cheese

Directions:

Heat butter in a frying pan over medium-high heat. Add sausages and cook, turning, for about 5 minutes or until cooked through. Thinly slice.

Spread cream cheese over 4 slices of bread. Add sprouts, cheddar, sausage, and tomatoes. Top with remaining bread, cut in half and serve.

Eggs Baked in Tomato Sauce

Serves 2

Ingredients:

1 small onion, finely cut

1 garlic clove, chopped

1 red pepper, chopped

2 eggs

1 can tomatoes, diced and undrained

1/2 tsp dried oregano

1/2 tsp cumin

2 tbsp olive oil

salt and black pepper, to taste

2 tbsp grated Parmesan cheese

Directions:

In a skillet, sauté onion and pepper over medium heat, untill soft. Add garlic and cook until just fragrant.

Stir in the tomatoes and bring to a boil. Crack 2 eggs into the skillet and season with, salt, pepper, oregano and cumin.

Sprinkle the cheese over the eggs and cook the for about 10 minutes, until the whites are just set. Serve with toast.

Mediterranean Scrambled Eggs

Serves 5-6

Ingredients:

1 small onion, finely cut

1 green bell pepper, chopped

1 red bell pepper, chopped

2 tomatoes, diced

1 garlic clove, pressed

8 eggs

10 oz feta cheese, crumbled

4 tbsp olive oil

1/2 cup finely cut parsley

black pepper, to taste

salt, to taste

Directions:

In a large pan sauté onion over medium heat, till transparent. Reduce heat and add bell peppers and garlic. Continue cooking until soft.

Add the tomatoes and continue simmering until the mixture is almost dry. Add the cheese and all eggs, stir, and cook until well mixed and not too liquid.

Season with black pepper and remove from heat. Sprinkle with parsley.

Salami Scrambled Eggs

Serves 5-6

Ingredients:

1 small onion, finely cut

1 cup thickly sliced salami, cut into 1/4-inch strips

2 cups baby rocket leaves, torn

8 eggs

4 tbsp olive oil

salt and black pepper, to taste

Directions:

In a large pan sauté onion over medium heat, till transparent. Reduce heat and add the salami strips. Cook, stirring occasionally, until lightly browned, about 2 minutes.

Add the rocket leaves and all eggs, stir, and cook until the eggs are softly set.

Season with salt and black pepper and remove from heat.

Mushroom and Spinach Scrambled Eggs

Serves 5-6

Ingredients:

1 small onion, finely cut

3 cups white mushrooms, thinly sliced

4 cups baby spinach, torn

8 eggs

2 tbsp butter

salt and black pepper, to taste

3 tbsp Parmesan cheese, to serve

Directions:

In a large pan, sauté onion and mushrooms in butter, over medium heat, untill soft, about 7 min. Add the spinach and stir until wilted. Season with salt and pepper.

Add in the eggs, stir, and cook until the eggs are softly set. Sprinkle with Parmesan cheese and serve.

Feta and Olive Scrambled Eggs

Serves 4

Ingredients:

5-6 green onions, finely cut

10 oz feta cheese, crumbled

1 cup black olives, pitted and halved

8 eggs

2 tbsp olive oil

1/2 tsp dried oregano

salt and black pepper, to taste

Directions:

In a large pan, sauté the onions in olive oil, over medium heat, untill soft, about 1-2 min.

Add the cheese and all eggs, stir, and cook until well mixed and not too liquid.

Stir in the olives and oregano, cook for a minute more, and serve.

Cornmeal Avocado Muffins

Serves: 12

Ingredients:

1 cup whole wheat flour

1 cup cornmeal

1/4 cup brown sugar

3 large eggs

1 tsp baking powder

1 tsp baking soda

1 tsp salt

1 cup milk

1/2 cup mashed avocado

1/2 cup Cheddar cheese

Directions:

Preheat oven to 375 F. Grease 12 muffin tin wells or line with paper cups.

In a large bowl, whisk together the cornmeal, whole wheat flour, sugar, baking powder, baking soda, and salt.

In a separate bowl, whisk together the eggs, milk and mashed avocado. Combine with avocado mixture; do not over-mix. Stir in 1/2 cup Cheddar cheese.

Spoon batter into prepared muffin tin; bake 15-18 minutes or until tops start to brown and a toothpick inserted into a muffin comes out clean.

Healthy Breakfast Muffins

Serves: 12

Ingredients:

1 cup whole wheat flour

1 cup plain flour

1/4 cup brown sugar

2 large eggs

1 tsp baking powder

1 tsp baking soda

1 tsp salt

1/2 tsp vanilla extract

1 cup yogurt

2 tbsp olive oil

1 cup mashed banana

1/2 cup pureed apples

2 tbsp mixed seeds (pumpkin, sunflower and flaxseed)

Directions:

Preheat oven to 375 F. Grease 12 muffin tin wells or line with paper cups.

In a large bowl, whisk together the flour, sugar, baking powder, baking soda, vanilla and salt.

In a separate bowl, whisk together the eggs, yogurt, olive oil, mashed banana and apple puree. Combine with dry mixture; do not over-mix.

Spoon batter into prepared muffin tin. Sprinkle the muffins with the seeds. Bake for 15-18 minutes or until tops start to brown and a toothpick inserted into a muffin comes out clean. Remove from the oven, transfer to a wire rack and leave to cool.

Marmalade Muffins

Serves: 9

Ingredients:

1 cup plain flour

1/4 cup brown sugar

1 large egg

2/3 cup orange juice

1/2 cup yogurt

1 tsp baking powder

1/2 tsp baking soda

1/2 tsp salt

1 tsp grated orange zest

1/2 tsp vanilla extract

1 tbsp sunflower oil

9 tsp marmalade

Directions:

Preheat oven to 375 F. Grease 9 muffin tin wells or line with paper cups.

In a large bowl, whisk together the flour, sugar, baking powder, baking soda, orange zest, vanilla and salt.

In a separate bowl, whisk together the egg, yogurt, oil and orange juice Combine with dry mixture; do not over-mix.

Spoon 1 tbsp of the mixture into each muffin case, top with 1 tsp of marmalade, then cover with the remaining muffin mix. Bake for 15-18 minutes or until tops start to brown and a toothpick inserted into a muffin comes out clean. Remove from the oven, transfer to a wire rack and leave to cool.

Semolina Dessert

Serves 5-6

Ingredients:

1 cup semolina

4 oz butter

2 tbsp pine nuts

for the syrup:

1 cup sugar

1 cup water

1 cup milk

Directions:

Mix semolina, butter and pine nuts in a large pot and cook them, stirring constantly, on medium-low heat until golden brown.

In another pot, mix the syrup ingredients and bring to the boil.

Very slowly pour the syrup into the pot with the semolina, stirring with a spoon, for 4-5 minutes, or until the mixture leaves the sides of the pot.

Remove from the heat and set aside, covered, for 5 minutes. When cooled, put on a plate upside down and serve in slices.

Coconut-flavored Rice Pudding with Figs

Serves 4

Ingredients:

1 1/2 cups short-grain white rice, rinsed

1/2 cup brown sugar

8 figs, halved

3 cups boiling water

1 1/2 cups shredded coconut

1 tsp salt

1 tbsp vanilla powder

Directions:

In a heavy saucepan, bring 1 ½ cup water to a boil, then add the rice, stirring, until it boils again. Reduce the heat and simmer for 7-8 minutes, until the water is absorbed and the rice is half-cooked.

In another bowl, pour 1/12 cups boiling water over the shredded coconut, sugar, and vanilla and let it soak for 20 minutes. Drain well and pour into the rice. Bring to a boil, reduce the heat and simmer until the rice is done. Stir in the figs and serve.

Pasta with Honey and Pistachios

Serves 2

Ingredients:

1 cup cooked small pasta, warm

1 tbsp pistachio nuts, finely ground

1 tbsp butter

2 tbsp honey

3 tbsp sugar

1/2 tsp orange zest

1/2 tsp rose water

Directions:

Combine well all the ingredients in a bowl and serve warm or room temperature.

Yogurt-Strawberry Ice Pops

Serves 8-9

Ingredients:

3 cups yogurt

3 tbsp honey

2 cups strawberries, quartered

Directions:

Strain the yogurt in a piece of cheesecloth or a clean white dishtowel. You can suspend it over a bowl or the sink. Combine the strained yogurt with honey.

Blend the strawberries with a blender then gently fold the strawberry puree into the yogurt mixture until just barely combined, with streaks remaining. Divide evenly among the molds, insert the sticks and freeze for 3 to 4 hours until solid.

Blueberry Yogurt Dessert

Serves 6

Ingredients:

1/3 cup blueberry jam

1 cup fresh blueberries

2 tbsp powdered sugar

1 cup heavy cream

2 cups yogurt

1 tsp vanilla extract

Directions:

Strain the yogurt in a piece of cheesecloth or a clean white dishtowel. You can suspend it over a bowl or the sink.

In a large bowl, beat the cream and powdered sugar until soft peaks form. Add strained yogurt and vanilla and beat until medium peaks form and the mixture is creamy and thick.

Gently fold half the fresh blueberries and the blueberry jam into cream mixture until just barely combined, with streaks remaining. Divide dessert among 6 glass bowls, top with fresh blueberries and serve.

Date Pinwheels

Serves 40-50

Ingredients:

3 1/2 cups flour

1 cup butter, softened

1 1/2 cups sugar

1 cup brown sugar

3 eggs, whisked

1 tsp lemon zest

1/2 tsp salt

1 tsp vanilla extract

1 1/2 tsp baking soda

2 cups dates, pitted and chopped

½ cup water

1 cup walnuts, chopped

Directions:

Chop the dates and place them in a saucepan with the water and 1/2 cup sugar. Simmer gently over medium heat until the mixture is thick. Add lemon zest and chopped nuts. Mix well and let cool.

Cream together the butter, sugar and brown sugar until light and fluffy. Whisk eggs until thick and add them to the butter mixture, incorporating them well. Stir in 1 teaspoon of vanilla extract. In a separate bowl, sift the flour together with salt and baking soda. Add that to the butter mixture and stir until just combined.

Divide dough into 3 parts. Roll out 1 part at a time into a rectangle. Spread a thin layer of date filling. Roll up jelly roll fashion in waxed paper. Refrigerate for at least one hour.

Preheat the oven to 350 F. Slice the rolls into 1/4 inch thick cookies using a sharp knife and arrange them 2 inch apart on greased or lined with parchment paper baking sheets.

Bake for 10-12 minutes, or until golden around the edges. Let cool on baking sheets for 10 minutes, then remove to wire racks. When completely cooled, store in airtight containers.

Date and Walnut Cookies

Serves 30

Ingredients:

2 cups flour

1/4 cup sour cream

1/2 cup butter, softened

1 1/2 cups brown sugar

1/2 cup white sugar

1 egg

1 cup dates, pitted and chopped

1/3 cup water

1/4 cup walnuts, finely chopped

1/2 tsp salt

1/2 tsp baking soda

a pinch of cinnamon

Directions:

Cook the dates together with the white sugar and water over medium-high heat, stirring constantly, until mixture is thick like jam. Add in the nuts, stir and remove from heat. Leave to cool.

In a medium bowl, beat the butter and brown sugar. Stir in the egg and the sour cream. Sift the flour together with salt, baking soda and cinnamon and stir it into the butter mixture.

Drop a teaspoon of dough onto a cookie sheet, place 1/4 teaspoon of the filling on top of it and top with an additional 1/2 teaspoon of dough. Repeat with the rest of the dough. Bake cookies for about 10 minutes in a preheated to 340 F oven, or until golden.

Turkish Delight Cookies

Serves 48

Ingredients:

4 cups flour

3/4 cup sugar

1 cup lard (or butter)

3 eggs

1 tsp baking powder

1 tsp vanilla extract

8 oz Turkish delight, chopped

powdered sugar, for dusting

Directions:

Heat oven to 375 F. Line baking sheets with parchment paper. Beat the eggs well, adding sugar a bit at a time. Beat for at least 3 minutes, until light and fluffy. Melt the lard, then let it cool enough and slowly combine it with the egg mixture.

Mix the flour and the baking powder. Gently add the flour mixture to the egg and lard mixture to create a smooth dough. Divide dough into two or three smaller balls and roll it out until ¼ inch thick. Cut squares 3x2 inch.

Place a piece of Turkish delight in each square, roll each cookie into a stick and nip the end. Bake in a preheated to 350 F oven until light pink. Dust in powdered sugar and store in an airtight container when completely cool.

FREE BONUS RECIPES:
10 Natural Homemade Body Scrubs and Beauty Recipes

Dry Skin Body Scrub

Ingredients:

½ cup brown sugar

½ cup sea salt salt

2-3 tbsp honey

2 tbsp argan oil

2 tbsp fresh orange juice

Directions:

Mix all ingredients until you have a smooth paste. Apply to wet skin and exfoliate body in small, circular motions. Rinse with warm water.

Lavender Body Scrub Recipe

Ingredients:

1/2 cup sugar

2 tbsp lavender leaves

¼ cup jojoba oil

3 drops lavender essential oil

Directions:

Combine sugar and lavender leaves. Add jojoba oil and lavender essential oil. Apply the mixture to damp skin. Gently exfoliate in small, circular motions. Rinse with warm water.

Rosemary Body Scrub

Ingredients:

1/2 cup coconut oil

1/2 cup sugar

1/4 cup flax seeds

7-8 drops Rosemary Essential Oil

Directions:

Combine sugar and flax seeds and stir until mixed well. Add the coconut oil and mix until evenly combined. Apply the mixture to damp skin. Gently exfoliate in small, circular motions. Rinse with warm water.

Banana-Sugar Body Scrub

Ingredients:

1 ripe banana

4 tbsp raw sugar

1 tbsp cocoa powder

2 tbsp almond oil

¼ tsp pure vanilla extract

Directions:

Smash ingredients together with a fork. Gently massage over your body for a few minutes. Rinse off with warm water

Coffee Body Scrub

Ingredients:

1/4 cup ground coffee

1/4 cup sugar

3 tbsp olive oil

1 vitamin E capsule

Directions:

Mix sugar with ground coffee, olive oil and the Vitamin E capsule. Apply over wet body and massage gently. Rinse off with warm water.

Strained Yogurt Face Mask

Ingredients:

5 tbsp plain yogurt

1 slice of white bread

Directions:

This is a very old family recipe and is also the easiest basic face mask. It was used probably by every Bulgarian mother and grandmother back in the days when there were no commercial creams and moisturizers.

Place the slice of bread in a plate, put the yogurt on top of it, spread it evenly and leave in the fridge for a few hours or overnight. In the morning take the strained yogurt and spread it on your clean face, leave it for 20 minutes and rinse it with water. Results are always excellent.

Oats Bran Face Mask

Ingredients:

3 tbsp oats bran

hot water

2 drops Bulgarian rose essential oil

Directions:

Boil bran in 1/2 cup of water. Strain, cool, add rose oil and apply to face. Leave for 15 minutes and wash with lukewarm water.

Pear and Honey Mask

Ingredients:

1 ripe pear

1 tbsp honey

1 tsp sour cream

Directions:

Peel and cut the pear, then mash it with a fork into a smooth paste. Stir in a tablespoon of honey and a teaspoon of cream. Spread the mixture evenly over your face and neck. Leave it for 10 minutes then rinse off.

Banana Nourishing Mask

Ingredients:

1 banana

1 tsp honey

1 tsp plain yogurt

Directions:

Mash a banana, add the honey and the yogurt, mix well and spread it evenly on a clean face. Leave it for at least 15 minutes and wash with cold water.

Apple Autumn Mask

Ingredients:

1/2 apple

1 tsp oatmeal

1 tsp honey

Directions:

Take a ripe half apple, grate it and mash it with a fork. Add one teaspoon oatmeal and one teaspoon honey to it and stir well. Spread on face and leave it on until the mixture dries completely then rinse it off with ordinary water.

About the Author

Vesela lives in Bulgaria with her family of six (including the Jack Russell Terrier). Her passion is going green in everyday life and she loves to prepare homemade cosmetic and beauty products for all her family and friends.

Vesela has been publishing her cookbooks for over a year now. If you want to see other healthy family recipes that she has published, together with some natural beauty books, you can check out her Author Page on Amazon.

Made in the USA
Middletown, DE
21 December 2018